GREAT
MICROWAVE
MEALS

GREAT
MICROWAVE
MEALS

Carol Bowen

SELECT
EDITIONS

Select Editions imprint specially produced for Selectabooks Ltd.

Produced by Anness Publishing Limited

ISBN 1 84081 073 4

© Anness Publishing Limited 1998

A CIP catalogue record for this book is available from the British Library.

Publisher: Joanna Lorenz
Executive Editor: Linda Fraser
Designer: William Mason
Jacket Designer: Ruth Hope
Illustrator: Madeleine David
Photography: Karl Adamson, Edward Allwright, David Armstrong, Steve Baxter,
James Duncan, Amanda Heywood and David Jordan
Recipes: Catherine Atkinson, Carol Bowen, Janet Brinkworth, Maxine Clarke, Christine France,
Sarah Gates, Shehzad Husain, Judy Jackson, Manisha Kanani, Sue Maggs, Elizabeth Martin,
Annie Nichols, Maggie Pannell, Jenny Stacey, Hilaire Walden and Elizabeth Wolf-Cohen

Printed and bound in Singapore

1 3 5 7 9 10 8 6 4 2

Previously published as part of a larger compendium.

Notes
For all recipes, quantities are given in both metric and imperial measures and, where
appropriate, measures are also given in standard cups and spoons. Follow one set, but
not a mixture, because they are not interchangeable.

Standard spoon and cup measures are level.
1 tsp = 5ml, 1 tbsp = 15ml, 1 cup = 250ml/8fl oz

Australian standard tablespoons are 20ml. Australian readers should use 3 tsp in place
of 1 tbsp for measuring small quantities of gelatine, cornflour, salt, etc.

Medium eggs are used unless otherwise stated

CONTENTS

Introduction

Undeniably, speed is the main advantage of microwave cooking; however, microwaves also make light work of cooking many staple dishes and family favourites. With a microwave cooker, vegetables, fruit-based desserts and many meat, fish and poultry dishes emerge from the microwave fresh, colourful, nutritionally rich and, moreover, most appetizing. The time-saving aspect may be great, as when cooking a jacket potato in about six minutes, or minimal, for example in the case of rice and pasta, but the additional benefit is being able to cook foods with the minimum attention and to just the right degree, be it *al dente*, tender-crisp, fork-tender or succulently moist.

ADVANTAGES OF MICROWAVE COOKING

SPEED
You can reduce normal cooking times by up to 75 per cent.

NUTRIENT RETENTION
Nutrient loss from food is often associated with other cooking methods. With microwave cooking, since timings are short and cooking liquid is minimal, there is less likely to be a loss of nutrients.

ECONOMY
Since microwaves do not involve preheating, and food cooks for a shorter time, it saves money on energy bills.

FEW COOKING SMELLS
Cooking odours are usually contained within the microwave.

COOL KITCHEN
The microwave oven, dishes and the kitchen all stay cool, while only the food becomes hot.

LESS RISK OF BURNS
Since dishes only get hot by the conduction of heat from the food, there is less risk of getting a burn either from the dishes or from the oven.

LESS CLEANING AND WASHING UP
It is possible to cook and serve in the same container, which reduces the amount of washing up. Cleaning the cooker is also easier as food does not bake on as it does in conventional ovens and hobs.

SELECTING FOOD FOR MICROWAVE COOKING

Apart from a few restrictions, virtually any food can be cooked in the microwave, but there are some foods that cook better than others.

FISH AND SHELLFISH
Whether fresh or frozen, whole or filleted, plain-cooked or in a sauce, microwave-cooked fish and shellfish are hard to beat for ease of preparation.

Whole Fish Slit the skin in two or three places on whole fish to prevent it from bursting during cooking. The tail may need protecting for half the cooking time by shielding with a little foil.

Fillets, Steaks and Portions For best results, roll fillets into an even shape and secure with a wooden cocktail stick. Cover tightly during cooking. Fish steaks and pieces should be cooked with the thicker parts to the outer edge of the dish.

Coated Portions Breadcrumb-coated and battered fish can be cooked in the microwave – cook them in a microwave browning dish for best results.

Shellfish Most shellfish cook superbly. Always start with the minimum cooking time.

POULTRY AND GAME

Whole birds, quarters, portions, stir-fried strips and medallions of poultry and game can be cooked with good results. Portions cooked in a sauce are most successful.

Whole Birds Truss well to give a compact shape. Protect wing tips and drumstick bone ends with small pieces of foil for part of the cooking time. Start cooking whole birds breast-side down and turn over halfway through cooking. Place on a microwave rack to lift the bird above the cooking juices.

Large birds will brown slightly; smaller birds and portions can be browned under a hot grill after microwave cooking.

When cooking stuffed birds, add an extra 1 minute per 450g/1lb to the times recommended in cooking charts. After cooking, leave to stand, covered in foil.

Small Birds and Portions Small birds and poultry portions should be cooked skin-side up, with the thicker parts towards the outside of the dish. They will brown more readily if cooked in a roasting bag.

MEAT

With careful consideration of the quality and cut, meat cooked in the microwave is a great success.

Longer-cooking cuts can be microwaved with some success, but the microwave performs better with prime-quality cuts. With the exception of roast pork, do not salt meat before microwave cooking as this toughens the meat.

Joints Choose joints that are symmetrically shaped – bone and roll joints like legs and shoulders.

Minced Meat Minced beef, lamb and pork cook magnificently, whether as burgers or in a sauce. Meatloaves should be made in a ring mould for faster cooking.

Cubed Meat Cut cubes of meat for dishes such as casseroles into uniformly sized pieces to ensure even cooking. Reduce the liquid by up to a third as there is little evaporation in microwave cooking.

Sausages, Bacon and Kebabs Sausages, bacon and other fatty meats cook quickly with some degree of browning; cover with kitchen paper during cooking to prevent fat from splattering. Use wooden skewers for kebabs.

VEGETABLES

Only the minimum amount of water is used, so vegetables are colourful and tender-crisp. Add salt after cooking, as salt sprinkled on to vegetables can make them tough.

Whole Vegetables Potatoes, aubergines and tomatoes need pricking before cooking to prevent

them from bursting. Jacket potatoes will have a crisper, drier skin if cooked on a sheet of kitchen paper. Whole vegetables should be positioned so that the thicker parts are towards the outer edge of the dish.

Cut Vegetables These should be cut into even-size pieces and placed in a cook bag or covered dish. Stir, rearrange or shake the vegetables halfway through the cooking time.

FRUIT

Fruits can be baked, poached or stuffed with a sweetened filling.

Whole Fruit These must be scored or pricked if they are not peeled, so that the skin does not burst.

Dried Fruit Dried fruit can be cooked quickly to make compotes.

Pasta, Rice, Grains and Pulses The microwave makes light work of rehydrating beans and pulses, reducing soaking to about 1½ hours.

The time savings with cooking pasta, rice, grains and pulses are negligible, but the bonus is that they require little or no attention during cooking.

SOUPS AND STARTERS

Beef Chilli Soup

This hearty dish, based on a traditional chilli recipe, is excellent with fresh crusty bread as a warming start to any meal.

INGREDIENTS

Serves 4

15ml/1 tbsp oil

1 onion, chopped

175g/6oz/1½ cups minced beef

2 garlic cloves, chopped

1 red chilli, sliced

25g/1oz/2 tbsp plain flour

400g/14oz can chopped tomatoes

600ml/1 pint/2½ cups hot beef stock

222g/8oz/2 cups canned red kidney
  beans, drained

30ml/2 tbsp chopped fresh parsley

salt and ground black pepper

1 Place the oil and onion in a microwaveproof bowl. Microwave on HIGH for 2 minutes, stirring once. Mix in the beef and microwave on HIGH for 4−4½ minutes, stirring twice.

2 Add the garlic, chilli and flour. Microwave on HIGH for 1 minute, stirring once.

3 Add the tomatoes and stock, mixing well. Cover and microwave on HIGH for 8 minutes, stirring twice.

4 Stir in the red kidney beans and season well with salt and pepper. Cover and microwave on HIGH for 10 minutes, stirring halfway through cooking.

5 Add the chopped fresh parsley and check the seasoning, adjusting to taste. Serve the soup with crusty bread.

Chilled Leek and Potato Soup

This creamy, chilled soup is a version of the classic Vichyssoise, originally created by a French chef at the Ritz Carlton Hotel in New York to celebrate the opening of the roof gardens.

INGREDIENTS

Serves 4

25g/1oz/2 tbsp butter

15ml/1 tbsp vegetable oil

1 small onion, chopped

3 leeks, sliced

2 potatoes, diced

600ml/1 pint/2½ cups hot vegetable stock

300ml/½ pint/1¼ cups milk

45ml/3 tbsp single cream

a little extra milk (optional)

salt and ground black pepper

60ml/4 tbsp natural yogurt and snipped chives, to garnish

1 Place the butter and oil in a large microwaveproof bowl, then add the onion, leeks and potatoes. Cover and microwave on HIGH for 10 minutes, stirring halfway through cooking. Stir in the stock and milk. Microwave on HIGH for a further 5–8 minutes, until the potatoes are tender.

2 Purée the vegetables and liquid in a blender or food processor until smooth. Return the soup to the bowl, stir in the cream and season well.

3 Leave the soup to cool and then chill it for 3–4 hours, or until really cold. You may need to add a little extra milk to thin the soup down as it will thicken slightly on cooling.

4 Serve the chilled soup in individual bowls, each topped with a tablespoon of natural yogurt and a sprinkling of snipped fresh chives.

Curried Parsnip Soup

The spices impart a delicious, mild curry flavour to sweet parsnips.

INGREDIENTS

Serves 4

25g/1oz/2 tbsp butter

1 garlic clove, crushed

1 onion, chopped

5ml/1 tsp ground cumin

5ml/1 tsp ground coriander

450g/1lb parsnips, (about 4) sliced

10ml/2 tsp medium curry paste

450ml/¾ pint/1⅞ cups hot chicken stock

450ml/¾ pint/1⅞ cups milk

60ml/4 tbsp soured cream

squeeze of lemon juice

salt and ground black pepper

chopped fresh coriander, to garnish

garlic and coriander naan bread, to serve

1 Place the butter in a large microwaveproof bowl with the garlic and onion. Cover the bowl and microwave on HIGH for 2 minutes. Stir in the spices and microwave on HIGH for a further 1 minute.

2 Add the parsnips and stir until well coated with butter. Then stir in the curry paste, followed by the stock. Cover and microwave on HIGH for 10–12 minutes, stirring halfway through cooking, until the parsnips are tender.

3 Purée the soup in a blender or food processor until smooth. Return the soup to the bowl and stir in the milk. Microwave on HIGH for 2–3 minutes, stirring halfway through cooking, then add 30ml/2 tbsp of the soured cream, the lemon juice and seasoning to taste.

4 Stir the fresh coriander into the remaining soured cream and use to top each portion of soup. Serve with naan bread.

Cauliflower and Walnut Cream Soup

Even though cream is not added to this soup, the cauliflower gives it a delicious, rich, creamy texture.

Serves 4

1 medium cauliflower
1 onion, coarsely chopped
450ml/¾ pint/1⅞ cups hot chicken or
    vegetable stock
450ml/¾ pint/1⅞ cups skimmed milk
45ml/3 tbsp walnut pieces
salt and ground black pepper
paprika and chopped walnuts, to garnish

1 Trim the cauliflower of outer leaves and break it into small florets. Place the cauliflower, onion and stock in a large microwave-proof bowl.

2 Cover and microwave on HIGH for 8–10 minutes, stirring halfway through cooking, or until soft. Add the milk and walnuts, then purée in a food processor until smooth.

3 Return the soup to the bowl and season to taste. Microwave on HIGH for 2 minutes to reheat. Serve sprinkled with paprika and chopped walnuts.

VARIATIONS

To make Cauliflower and Almond Cream Soup, use 45ml/3 tbsp ground almonds in place of the walnut pieces.

Curried Carrot and Apple Soup

Serves 4

10ml/2 tsp sunflower oil
15ml/1 tbsp mild curry powder
500g/1¼lb carrots, chopped
1 large onion, chopped
1 cooking apple, cored and chopped
750ml/1¼ pints/3 cups hot chicken stock
salt and ground black pepper
natural low-fat yogurt and carrot curls,
    to garnish

COOK'S TIP

Choose an acidic apple that will soften and fluff up as it cooks. Chop it into fairly small pieces before adding to the bowl.

1 Place the oil in a large microwaveproof bowl. Add the curry powder and microwave on HIGH for 1 minute, stirring halfway through cooking.

2 Add the carrots, onion and apple, stir well, then cover and microwave on HIGH for 8–10 minutes, stirring halfway through cooking, until softened.

3 Spoon the vegetable mixture into a food processor or blender, then add half the stock and process until smooth.

4 Return the soup to the bowl and pour in the remaining stock. Microwave on HIGH for 3–4 minutes, stirring once, to reheat. Adjust the seasoning before serving in bowls, garnished with swirls of yogurt and a few curls of carrot.

Jerusalem Artichoke Soup

Topped with saffron cream, this soup is wonderful on a chilly day.

INGREDIENTS

Serves 4

50g/2oz/4 tbsp butter

1 onion, chopped

450g/1lb Jerusalem artichokes, peeled and
   cut into chunks

900ml/1½ pints/3¾ cups hot chicken
   stock

150ml/¼ pint/⅔ cup milk

150ml/¼ pint/⅔ cup double cream

good pinch of saffron powder

salt and ground black pepper

snipped fresh chives, to garnish

1 Place the butter and onion in a large microwaveproof bowl and microwave on HIGH for 2–3 minutes, until soft, stirring once.

2 Add the artichokes to the bowl and stir to coat them in the butter. Cover and microwave on HIGH for 8–10 minutes, stirring halfway through cooking. Pour in the stock and milk, then cover and microwave on HIGH for 5–8 minutes, stirring once. Cool slightly, then process in a blender or food processor until smooth.

3 Strain the soup back into the bowl. Add half the cream, season to taste, and microwave on HIGH for 2–3 minutes to reheat. Lightly whip the remaining cream with the saffron powder. Ladle the soup into warmed soup bowls and put a spoonful of saffron cream in the centre of each. Scatter over the snipped chives and serve at once.

Broccoli and Stilton Soup

A really easy, but rich, soup – choose something simple to follow, such as plainly roasted or grilled meat, poultry or fish.

INGREDIENTS

Serves 4

350g/12oz broccoli

25g/1oz/2 tbsp butter

1 onion, chopped

1 leek, white part only, chopped

1 small potato, cut into chunks

600ml/1 pint/2½ cups hot chicken stock

300ml/½ pint/1¼ cups milk

45ml/3 tbsp double cream

115g/4oz Stilton cheese, rind removed,
   crumbled

salt and ground black pepper

1 Break the broccoli into florets, discarding tough stems. Set aside two small florets for garnishing the soup.

2 Place the butter in a large microwaveproof bowl with the onion and leek. Microwave on HIGH for 3 minutes, until soft. Add the broccoli and potato, then pour in the stock. Cover and microwave on HIGH for 12–15 minutes, stirring twice, until the vegetables are tender.

3 Cool slightly, then purée in a blender or food processor. Strain through a sieve back into the bowl.

4 Add the milk, cream and seasoning to the bowl and microwave on HIGH for 3–4 minutes to reheat. At the last minute, add the cheese and stir until it just melts.

5 Place the reserved broccoli florets in a small microwave-proof bowl, cover and microwave on HIGH for 30 seconds, then cut them vertically into thin slices. Ladle the soup into warmed bowls. Garnish with the broccoli florets and serve with a generous grinding of black pepper.

Artichoke and Mushroom Soup

Delicate Jerusalem artichokes are perfectly matched with mushrooms in this simple soup. Select closed-cap mushrooms for good colour and light flavour.

INGREDIENTS

Serves 4

30–60ml/2–4 tbsp butter

115g/4oz/2 cups mushrooms, sliced

2 onions, chopped

450g/1lb Jerusalem artichokes, peeled and sliced

300ml/½ pint/1¼ cups hot vegetable stock

300ml/½ pint/1¼ cups milk

salt and ground black pepper

1 Place the butter and mushrooms in a large microwaveproof bowl. Cover and microwave on HIGH for 2 minutes. Using a slotted spoon, lift out the mushrooms and reserve on a plate. Add the onions and artichokes to the bowl, mixing well. Cover and microwave on HIGH for 8–10 minutes, stirring halfway through cooking.

2 Add the vegetable stock to the bowl and microwave on HIGH for a further 5 minutes, until the artichokes are soft, then season to taste.

3 Purée the soup in a blender or food processor, adding the milk slowly until smooth. Return the soup to the bowl. Stir in the mushrooms and microwave on HIGH for 2–3 minutes to reheat before serving.

Tomato and Red Pepper Soup

A late summer soup that can be served cold. Made using very ripe peppers and tomatoes, it won't be nearly as tasty if made with winter vegetables that have not been ripened in the sun.

INGREDIENTS

Serves 4

5 large tomatoes

30–60ml/2–4 tbsp olive oil

1 onion, chopped

450g/1lb thinly sliced red or orange peppers

30ml/2 tbsp tomato purée

a pinch of sugar

475ml/16fl oz/2 cups hot vegetable stock

60ml/4 tbsp soured cream (optional)

salt and ground black pepper

chopped fresh dill, to garnish

1 Skin the tomatoes by plunging them into boiling water for 30 seconds. Chop the flesh and reserve any juice.

2 Place half the oil in a microwaveproof bowl with the onion. Microwave on HIGH for 2 minutes, stirring once. Add the peppers and the remaining oil, mixing well. Cover and microwave on HIGH for 5 minutes, stirring halfway through cooking.

3 Stir in the chopped tomatoes, tomato purée, seasoning, sugar and a few tablespoons of stock. Cover and microwave on HIGH for 4 minutes, stirring halfway through cooking, until the vegetables are tender.

4 Stir in the rest of the stock and purée in a blender or food processor until smooth. Strain the soup to remove the skins and season to taste.

5 Pour into bowls, swirl in the soured cream, if using, and garnish with dill.

Chicken Liver Pâté with Marsala

This pâté is really quick and simple to make, yet it has a delicious – and quite sophisticated – flavour. It contains Marsala, a soft and pungent fortified wine from Sicily. Brandy or a medium-dry sherry may be used instead.

INGREDIENTS

Serves 4

350g/12oz chicken livers, defrosted
   if frozen
225g/8oz/1 cup butter, softened
2 garlic cloves, crushed
15ml/1 tbsp Marsala
5ml/1 tsp chopped fresh sage
salt and ground black pepper
8 sage leaves, to garnish
Melba toast, to serve

1 Trim any membranes and sinew from the livers, then rinse and dry with kitchen paper. Place 25g/1oz/2 tbsp of the butter in a microwaveproof bowl with the chicken livers and the garlic. Cover loosely and microwave on HIGH for about 4 minutes, or until the livers are firm, but pink in the middle, stirring twice.

2 Use a slotted spoon to transfer the livers to a blender or food processor. Add the Marsala and chopped sage.

3 Place 150g/5oz/10 tbsp of the remaining butter in a microwaveproof bowl and microwave on HIGH for 1½ minutes to melt, then pour it into the blender or processor and blend until smooth. Season well.

4 Spoon the pâté into four individual pots and smooth the surface. Place the remaining butter in a microwaveproof bowl and microwave on HIGH for 1 minute to melt and pour it over the pâtés. Garnish with sage leaves and chill until set. Serve with triangles of Melba toast.

COOK'S TIP

To make Melba toast, toast medium-thick bread. Cut off the crusts and slice the toast in half horizontally. Lightly brown the untoasted sides. Cool on a wire rack.

Leeks with Mustard Dressing

Pencil-slim baby leeks are increasingly available, and are beautifully tender. Use three or four of these smaller leeks per serving.

Serves 4

8 slim leeks, each about 13cm/5in long
45ml/3 tbsp water
5–10ml/1–2 tsp Dijon mustard
10ml/2 tsp white wine vinegar
1 hard-boiled egg, halved lengthways
75ml/5 tbsp light olive oil
10ml/2 tsp chopped fresh parsley
salt and ground black pepper

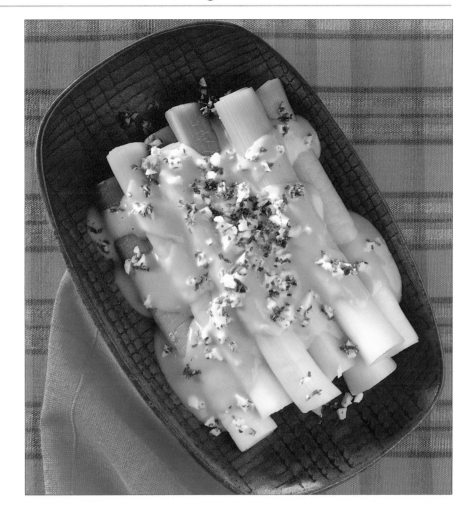

1 Place the leeks in a microwaveproof dish with the water. Cover and microwave on HIGH for 3–5 minutes, rearranging twice. Leave to stand for 2 minutes, then drain thoroughly.

2 Meanwhile, stir the mustard and vinegar together in a bowl. Scoop the egg yolk into the bowl and mash it thoroughly into the vinegar mixture using a fork.

3 Gradually work in the oil to make a smooth sauce, then season to taste.

4 Place the leeks on several layers of kitchen paper, then pat them dry with several more layers of kitchen paper.

5 Transfer the leeks to a serving dish. While they are still warm, spoon the dressing over them and leave to cool. Finely chop the egg white, then mix it with the chopped fresh parsley and scatter this over the leeks. Chill until ready to serve.

COOK'S TIP

Although this dish is served cold, make sure that the leeks are still warm when you pour over the dressing so that they will absorb the mustard flavours.

FISH AND SEAFOOD

Monkfish with Mexican Salsa

Serves 4

675g/1½lb monkfish tail

45ml/3 tbsp olive oil

30ml/2 tbsp lime juice

1 garlic clove, crushed

15ml/1 tbsp chopped fresh coriander ·

salt and ground black pepper

coriander sprigs and lime slices, to garnish

For the salsa

4 tomatoes, peeled, seeded and diced

1 avocado, peeled, stoned and diced

½ red onion, chopped

1 green chilli, seeded and chopped

30ml/2 tbsp chopped fresh coriander

30ml/2 tbsp olive oil

15ml/1 tbsp lime juice

1 Prepare the monkfish. Using a sharp knife, remove the pinkish-grey membrane. Cut one fillet from either side of the backbone, then cut both fillets in half to make four steaks.

2 Mix together the oil, lime juice, garlic, coriander and seasoning in a shallow non-metallic dish. Add the monkfish steaks and turn them several times to coat with the marinade. Cover the dish and leave the fish to marinate at cool room temperature, or in the fridge, for several hours.

3 About 30 minutes before cooking the fish, mix all the salsa ingredients and leave to marinate at room temperature.

4 Remove the monkfish from the marinade and place in a shallow microwaveproof dish. Cover and microwave on HIGH for 4–6 minutes, turning once and brushing twice with the marinade, until cooked through.

5 Serve the monkfish garnished with coriander sprigs and lime slices and accompanied by the salsa.

COOK'S TIP

It is important to remove the tough, pinkish-grey membrane covering the monkfish tail before cooking, otherwise it will shrink and toughen the monkfish.

Herby Fish Cakes with Lemon-Chive Sauce

The wonderful flavour of fresh herbs makes these fish cakes the catch of the day.

INGREDIENTS

Serves 4

350g/12oz potatoes, peeled
60ml/4 tbsp water
75ml/5 tbsp skimmed milk
350g/12oz haddock or hoki fillets, skinned
15ml/1 tbsp lemon juice
15ml/1 tbsp creamed horseradish sauce
30ml/2 tbsp chopped fresh parsley
flour, for dusting
115g/4oz/2 cups fresh wholemeal bread-
     crumbs
salt and ground black pepper
sprig of flat leaf parsley, to garnish
mangetouts and a sliced tomato and
     onion salad, to serve

For the lemon-chive sauce
thinly pared rind and juice of ½ small
     lemon
120ml/4fl oz/½ cup dry white wine
2 thin slices fresh root ginger
10ml/2 tsp cornflour
30ml/2 tbsp snipped fresh chives

1 Cut the potatoes into small cubes and place in a microwaveproof bowl with 45ml/3 tbsp of the water. Cover and microwave on HIGH for 6–8 minutes until tender, stirring halfway through cooking. Drain and mash with the milk and season to taste.

2 Purée the fish with the lemon juice and horseradish sauce in a blender or food processor, then mix the purée with the potatoes and parsley.

3 With floured hands, shape the mixture into eight cakes and coat them with the breadcrumbs. Chill the fish cakes for 30 minutes.

4 To make the sauce, cut the lemon rind into julienne strips and place it in a large microwave-proof bowl. Add the lemon juice, wine, ginger and seasoning to taste. Microwave on HIGH for 3–4 minutes, stirring twice.

5 Blend the cornflour with the remaining 15ml/1 tbsp cold water. Add to the sauce and stir until clear. If necessary, microwave on HIGH for 1 minute, stirring once, until clear and thickened.

6 To cook the fish cakes, place them in a shallow microwave-proof dish. Cover and microwave on HIGH for 7–8 minutes, turning the cakes over halfway through cooking. Brown lightly under a preheated hot grill, if liked.

7 Stir the chives into the hot sauce and serve immediately with the fish cakes, garnished with sprigs of flat leaf parsley. Mangetouts and a sliced tomato and onion salad are suitable accompaniments.

Mackerel Kebabs with Parsley Dressing

Fish kebabs cook quickly and evenly in the microwave.

INGREDIENTS

Serves 4

450g/1lb mackerel fillets

finely grated rind and juice of 1 lemon

45ml/3 tbsp chopped fresh parsley

12 cherry tomatoes

8 black olives, stoned

salt and ground black pepper

1 Cut the fish into 4cm/1½in chunks and place in a bowl with half the lemon rind and juice, half the parsley and seasoning. Cover and leave to marinate for 30 minutes.

2 Thread the fish on to eight long wooden skewers, alternating the chunks with tomatoes and olives. Place the kebabs on a microwave-proof roasting rack or rest them across a shallow microwaveproof dish. Cover with greaseproof paper and microwave on HIGH for 4–6 minutes. Rearrange halfway through cooking, until the fish is cooked.

3 Mix the remaining lemon rind and juice with the remaining parsley in a small bowl, adding seasoning to taste. Spoon the dressing over the kebabs and serve hot, with plain boiled rice or noodles and a leafy green salad.

COOK'S TIP
∽

When using wooden or bamboo kebab skewers, soak them first in a bowl of cold water for a few minutes to help prevent them from drying out and cracking.

VARIATIONS

Other firm-fleshed fish may be used in place of the mackerel – for a special occasion you could opt for salmon fillet or monkfish tail; or try a mixture of the two, threading the fish chunks alternately on to the skewers with the tomatoes and olives.

Cod Creole

The lime or lemon juice and cayenne add piquancy to this dish.

Serves 4

450g/1lb cod fillet, skinned

15ml/1 tbsp lime or lemon juice

10ml/2 tsp olive oil

1 onion, finely chopped

1 green pepper, seeded and sliced

2.5ml/½ tsp cayenne pepper

2.5ml/½ tsp garlic salt

400g/14oz can chopped tomatoes

1 Cut the cod fillet into bite-sized chunks and sprinkle with the lime or lemon juice.

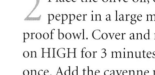

2 Place the olive oil, onion and pepper in a large microwave-proof bowl. Cover and microwave on HIGH for 3 minutes, stirring once. Add the cayenne pepper and garlic salt.

3 Stir in the cod with the chopped tomatoes and cover. Microwave on HIGH for 8–10 minutes, stirring twice, until the fish is cooked and flakes easily. Serve with boiled rice or potatoes.

COOK'S TIP

Be careful not to overcook the fish – or to let it bubble too vigorously in the sauce – as the chunks will break up.

Five-spice Fish

Chinese mixtures of spicy, sweet and sour flavours are particularly successful with fish – and dinner is ready in minutes!

Serves 4

5ml/1 tsp Chinese five-spice powder

20ml/4 tsp cornflour

4 portions white fish fillet, such as cod, haddock or hoki, about 175g/6oz each

15ml/1 tbsp sesame or sunflower oil

3 spring onions, shredded

5ml/1 tsp finely chopped fresh root ginger

150g/5oz button mushrooms, sliced

115g/4oz baby corn, sliced

30ml/2 tbsp soy sauce

45ml/3 tbsp dry sherry or apple juice

5ml/1 tsp sugar

salt and ground black pepper

1 Mix the five-spice powder and cornflour and use to coat the portions of fish.

2 Place the oil in a shallow microwaveproof dish with the spring onions, ginger, mushrooms and corn. Cover and microwave on HIGH for 2 minutes, stirring once. Add the fish and toss well to mix. Cover and microwave on HIGH for 4–6 minutes, stirring once.

3 Mix together the soy sauce, sherry or apple juice and sugar, then pour this mixture over the fish. Cover and microwave on HIGH for 2–3 minutes, stirring once. Adjust the seasoning, then serve with noodles and stir-fried vegetables.

Spaghetti with Seafood Sauce

For speed, the sauce for this recipe is cooked in the microwave while the spaghetti is cooked on the hob.

INGREDIENTS

Serves 4

45ml/3 tbsp olive oil

1 onion, chopped

1 garlic clove, finely chopped

225g/8oz spaghetti

600ml/1 pint/2½ cups passata

15ml/1 tbsp tomato purée

5ml/1 tsp dried oregano

1 bay leaf

5ml/1 tsp sugar

115g/4oz/1 cup peeled cooked shrimps,
  drained and well rinsed if canned

115g/4oz/1 cup peeled cooked prawns

175g/6oz/1½ cups shelled cooked clams or
  cockles, drained and well rinsed if
  canned or bottled

15ml/1 tbsp lemon juice

45ml/3 tbsp chopped fresh parsley

25g/1oz/2 tbsp butter

salt and ground black pepper

4 whole cooked prawns, to garnish
  (optional)

1 Place the oil in a microwave-proof bowl and add the onion and garlic. Microwave on HIGH for 3 minutes, stirring halfway through cooking.

2 Meanwhile, cook the spaghetti in a large saucepan of boiling salted water for 10–12 minutes until *al dente*.

3 Stir the passata, tomato purée, oregano, bay leaf and sugar into the onions and season well. Cover and microwave on HIGH for 4 minutes, stirring twice during cooking.

4 Add the shrimps, prawns, clams or cockles, lemon juice and 30ml/2 tbsp of the parsley. Stir well, then cover and microwave on HIGH for 3–4 minutes, stirring once, until the shellfish are heated through.

5 Meanwhile, drain the cooked spaghetti and add the butter to the pan. Return the drained spaghetti to the pan and toss it in the butter. Season well with ground black pepper.

6 Divide the spaghetti between four warmed plates and top with the seafood sauce. Sprinkle with the remaining parsley, garnish with whole prawns and serve immediately.

Stuffed Plaice Rolls

Plaice fillets are a good choice because they are delicate in flavour, easy to cook, and free of bones.

INGREDIENTS

Serves 4

2 carrots, grated

1 courgette, grated

60ml/4 tbsp fresh wholemeal
   breadcrumbs

15ml/1 tbsp lime or lemon juice

4 plaice fillets

salt and ground black pepper

1 Mix together the grated carrots and courgette. Stir in the breadcrumbs, lime or lemon juice and seasoning.

2 Lay the fish fillets skin side up and divide the stuffing between them, spreading it evenly.

3 Roll up the fillets to enclose the stuffing and place in a microwaveproof dish. Cover and microwave on HIGH for 4–6 minutes, rearranging once. Leave to stand, covered, for 3 minutes before serving. Serve hot with new potatoes.

COOK'S TIP

The plaice rolls create their own delicious juices, but for additional sauce, stir chopped fresh parsley into a little low-fat fromage frais and serve this with the fish.

VARIATIONS

Lemon sole can be used instead of plaice. Alternatively, buy thick pieces of cod or salmon fillet and simply top them with the carrot and courgette mixture. The microwave cooking times will be a little longer if cod steaks are used.

Spiced Fish with Okra

INGREDIENTS

Serves 4

450g/1lb monkfish

5ml/1 tsp ground turmeric

2.5ml/½ tsp chilli powder

2.5ml/½ tsp salt

5ml/1 tsp cumin seeds

2.5ml/½ tsp fennel seeds

2 dried red chillies

45ml/3 tbsp oil

1 onion, finely chopped

2 garlic cloves, crushed

4 tomatoes, skinned and finely chopped

150ml/¼ pint/⅔ cup water

225g/8oz okra, trimmed and cut into
   2.5cm/1in lengths

5ml/1 tsp garam masala

tomato rice, to serve

1 Remove the membrane and bones from the monkfish. Cut the fillet into 2.5cm/1in cubes and place them in a dish. Mix the turmeric, chilli powder and 1.5ml/¼ tsp of the salt, then rub this mixture all over the fish. Marinate the fish for 15 minutes.

2 Mix the cumin seeds, fennel seeds and chillies in a large microwaveproof bowl, cover and microwave on HIGH for 1–2 minutes. Transfer the spices to a blender or mortar and process or grind them to a coarse powder.

3 Place 30ml/2 tbsp of the oil in a large microwaveproof bowl and microwave on HIGH for 30 seconds, until hot. Add the fish, turning the pieces in the oil. Cover and microwave on HIGH for 4–5 minutes, stirring halfway through cooking. Use a slotted spoon to remove the fish from the bowl.

4 Add the remaining oil to the bowl with the onion, garlic, ground spice mixture and the remaining salt. Cover and microwave on HIGH for 2 minutes, stirring once. Stir in the tomatoes and water, cover and microwave on HIGH for 2–3 minutes, stirring once.

5 Add the okra, cover and microwave on HIGH for 4–6 minutes, stirring halfway through cooking.

6 Replace the fish. Add the garam masala and lightly mix both with the sauce. Cover and microwave on HIGH for 2–3 minutes, until the fish is hot and the okra is tender. Serve with rice flavoured with a little tomato purée during cooking.

COOK'S TIP

Yellow (flavoured with turmeric or saffron) and plain rice also go well with this spiced dish, and the two colours make an attractive presentation.

Coconut Salmon

This is an ideal dish to serve at dinner parties.

INGREDIENTS

Serves 4

10ml/2 tsp ground cumin

10ml/2 tsp chilli powder

2.5ml/½ tsp ground turmeric

30ml/2 tbsp white wine vinegar

1.5ml/¼ tsp salt

4 salmon steaks, about 175g/6oz each

45ml/3 tbsp oil

1 onion, chopped

2 green chillies, seeded and chopped

2 garlic cloves, crushed

2.5cm/1in piece fresh root ginger, grated

5ml/1 tsp ground coriander

175ml/6fl oz/¾ cup coconut milk

fresh coriander sprigs, to garnish

spring onion rice, to serve

1 Mix 5ml/1 tsp of the ground cumin with the chilli powder, turmeric, vinegar and salt. Rub this spice paste over the salmon steaks and leave to marinate for about 15 minutes.

2 Place the oil in a large, deep microwaveproof dish. Add the onion, chillies, garlic and ginger. Cover and microwave on HIGH for 3 minutes, stirring halfway though cooking. Process this cooked mixture to a paste in a food processor or blender.

3 Return the paste to the dish. Stir in the remaining cumin, the ground coriander and coconut milk. Microwave on HIGH for 2–2½ minutes, stirring twice during cooking.

4 Add the salmon steaks, cover and microwave on MEDIUM for 9–10 minutes, rearranging halfway through cooking, until the fish is cooked. Leave to stand for 5 minutes before serving, garnished with coriander. Serve rice flavoured with spring onions with the salmon.

COOK'S TIP

To make coconut milk, dissolve grated creamed coconut in boiling water and strain it into a jug, if necessary.

Ginger and Lime Prawns

INGREDIENTS

Serves 4

225g/8oz raw tiger prawns, peeled

⅓ cucumber

15ml/1 tbsp sunflower oil

15ml/1 tbsp sesame seed oil

175g/6oz mangetouts, trimmed

4 spring onions, diagonally sliced

30ml/2 tbsp chopped fresh coriander, to
garnish

For the marinade

15ml/1 tbsp clear honey

15ml/1 tbsp light soy sauce

15ml/1 tbsp dry sherry

2 garlic cloves, crushed

small piece of fresh root ginger, peeled
and finely chopped

juice of 1 lime

1 Mix the marinade ingredients,
stir in the prawns and leave to
marinate for 1–2 hours.

2 Prepare the cucumber: slice it
in half lengthways, scoop out
the seeds, then slice each half
neatly into crescents. Set aside.

3 Place both types of oil in a
large microwaveproof bowl.
Microwave on HIGH for
30 seconds. Drain the prawns
(reserving the marinade) and
add them to the oils. Cover and
microwave on HIGH for 1½–
2½ minutes, stirring halfway
through cooking, until they begin
to turn pink.

4 Add the mangetouts and the
cucumber, cover and
microwave on HIGH for a further
1–2 minutes, stirring once.

5 Stir in the reserved marinade
and microwave on HIGH for a
further 30 seconds. Stir in the
spring onions and serve, sprinkled
with fresh coriander.

Mediterranean Fish Cutlets

INGREDIENTS

Serves 4

4 white fish cutlets, about 150g/5oz each

45ml/3 tbsp fish stock

45ml/3 tbsp dry white wine

1 bay leaf, a few black peppercorns
and a strip of pared lemon rind,
for flavouring

chopped fresh parsley, to garnish

For the tomato sauce

400g/14oz can chopped tomatoes

1 garlic clove, crushed

15ml/1 tbsp sun-dried tomato paste

15ml/1 tbsp pastis or other aniseed-
flavoured liqueur

15ml/1 tbsp drained capers

12–16 black olives, stoned

salt and ground black pepper

1 To make the tomato sauce,
place the tomatoes, garlic,
tomato paste, pastis or liqueur,
capers, olives and salt and pepper
in a microwaveproof bowl. Cover
and microwave on HIGH for 4–6
minutes, stirring twice.

2 Place the fish cutlets in a
microwaveproof dish, pour
over the stock and wine and add
the flavourings. Cover and
microwave on HIGH for
5 minutes, rotating the dish twice.
Leave to stand for 2 minutes.

3 Using a slotted spoon, transfer
the fish to a heated dish. Strain
the stock into the tomato sauce
and mix well. Season the sauce,
pour it over the fish and serve
immediately, garnished with
chopped parsley.

MEAT AND
POULTRY

Beef and Lentil Pie

In this variation of cottage pie, lentils are substituted for some of the meat to produce a dish that is lower in fat and higher in fibre.

INGREDIENTS

Serves 4

175g/6oz/1 cup green lentils

1 onion, chopped

2 celery sticks, chopped

1 large carrot, chopped

1 garlic clove, crushed

225g/8oz lean minced beef

425g/15oz can chopped tomatoes

10ml/2 tsp yeast extract

1 bay leaf

For the topping

450g/1lb potatoes, peeled and cut into
    large chunks

450g/1lb parsnips, peeled and cut into
    large chunks

60ml/4 tbsp low-fat natural yogurt

45ml/3 tbsp snipped chives

20ml/4 tsp freshly grated Parmesan cheese

2 tomatoes, sliced

25g/1oz/¼ cup pine nuts (optional)

3 Drain the lentils, reserving 250ml/8fl oz/1 cup of the cooking water in a measuring jug. Add the lentils to the meat mixture, then dissolve the yeast extract in the cooking water and stir it in with the bay leaf. Cover loosely, then microwave on HIGH for 12–15 minutes, stirring twice.

1 Place the lentils in a microwave-proof bowl and pour in boiling water to cover. Cover and microwave on HIGH for 6 minutes.

2 Place onion, celery, carrot and garlic in a microwaveproof bowl. Cover, microwave on HIGH for 4 minutes and stir once. Add mince, stir and microwave on HIGH for 2 minutes. Mix in tomatoes.

4 Make the topping: place the potatoes and parsnips in a microwaveproof bowl with 75ml/5 tbsp water. Cover and microwave on HIGH for 11–13 minutes, stirring once, until tender. Mash the potatoes and parsnips together and stir in the yogurt and chives.

5 Remove the bay leaf and divide the meat mixture among four small dishes or one large dish suitable for grilling. Spoon over the potato mixture. Sprinkle with Parmesan and garnish with tomato slices. Scatter pine nuts over the top, if using, and grill the pies for a few minutes until the topping is crisp and golden brown.

Butterflied Cumin and Garlic Lamb

Ground cumin and garlic give the lamb a wonderful Middle-Eastern flavour. Vary the recipe by making a simple oil, lemon and herb marinade instead.

INGREDIENTS

Serves 6

1.75kg/4lb leg of lamb

60ml/4 tbsp olive oil

30ml/2 tbsp ground cumin

4–6 garlic cloves, crushed

salt and ground black pepper

pilaff with raisins and toasted almonds,
    to serve

coriander sprigs and lemon wedges,
    to garnish

1 To butterfly the lamb, cut away the meat from the bone using a small sharp knife. Remove any excess fat and the thin, parchment-like membrane. Bat out the meat to an even thickness, then prick the fleshy side well with a knife tip.

2 In a bowl, mix together the oil, cumin and garlic, and season with pepper. Spoon the mixture all over the lamb, then rub it well into the crevices. Cover and leave to marinate overnight.

3 Spread the lamb, skin-side down, on a microwave roasting rack or upturned saucer in a microwaveproof shallow dish. Season with salt and microwave on HIGH for 5 minutes. Reduce the power setting to MEDIUM and microwave for a further 30–35 minutes, or until the meat is cooked but still pink inside, turning it over once.

4 Brown the lamb under a preheated hot grill to crisp the outside, if liked. Leave to stand, covered with foil, for 10–15 minutes before carving.

5 Cut the lamb into diagonal slices and serve it with a rice pilaff with toasted almonds and raisins. Garnish with coriander sprigs and lemon wedges.

COMBINATION MICROWAVE

This recipe is suitable for cooking in a combination microwave. Follow the oven manufacturer's timing guide for good results.

Rack of Lamb with Redcurrant Bunches

Bunches of redcurrants tied with chives provide a strong colour contrast to glazed rack of lamb.

INGREDIENTS

Serves 4–6

45ml/3 tbsp redcurrant jelly

5ml/1 tsp wholegrain mustard

2 best ends of lamb, each with 6 chops, trimmed of all fat

120ml/4fl oz/½ cup red wine

120ml/4fl oz/½ cup stock or water

salt and ground black pepper

For the garnish

4–6 chives, wilted

8–12 small bunches of redcurrants

1 Place the redcurrant jelly with the mustard in a small microwaveproof bowl and microwave on HIGH for 1–2 minutes, stirring once, until the jelly has melted. Brush the mixture over the lamb.

2 Place the racks of lamb on a microwave roasting rack or upturned saucer in a microwave-proof shallow dish. Microwave on HIGH for 18–22 minutes, or until cooked to your taste, rotating the dish and basting the lamb four times during cooking. Transfer the lamb to a warm platter, loosely cover it with foil and allow to rest for 10 minutes.

3 Drain the fat from the roasting dish, leaving the sediment behind. Stir in the red wine and microwave on HIGH for 2–3 minutes, until most of the liquid has evaporated.

4 Add the stock or water. Microwave on HIGH for 3–4 minutes until reduced and very slightly syrupy. Season, strain into a sauceboat and keep hot.

5 Wrap the chives around the redcurrant stems, tie them in a neat knot and then trim the ends. Make four bunches of redcurrants in this way. Carve the lamb into cutlets, arrange them on four or six dinner plates and spoon over a little of the sauce. To complete the dish, garnish with the redcurrant bunches.

COMBINATION MICROWAVE

This recipe is suitable for cooking in a combination microwave. Follow the oven manufacturer's timing guide for good results.

Stilton Burgers

Slightly more up-market than the traditional burger, this tasty recipe contains a delicious surprise. The lightly melted Stilton cheese encased in a burger is absolutely delicious.

INGREDIENTS

Serves 4

450g/1lb/4 cups minced beef
1 onion, finely chopped
1 celery stick, chopped
5ml/1 tsp dried mixed herbs
5ml/1 tsp prepared mustard
50g/2oz/½ cup Stilton cheese, crumbled
4 burger buns
salt and ground black pepper

1 Place the minced beef in a bowl together with the onion and celery. Season well.

2 Stir in the herbs and mustard, bringing all the ingredients together to form a firm mixture.

3 Divide the mixture into eight equal portions. Place four on a chopping board and flatten each one slightly.

4 Share the crumbled cheese between the burgers, placing a little in the centre of each.

5 Flatten the remaining mixture and place on top. Mould the mixture to encase the crumbled cheese and shape into four burgers.

6 To cook, place the burgers on a microwaveproof roasting rack and microwave, uncovered, for 6–7 minutes, turning over once. Leave to stand for 2–3 minutes. Alternatively, for a browner and crisper result, preheat a microwave browning dish or special microwave burger cooker according to the manufacturer's instructions. Add the burgers, pressing them down well on to the base, and microwave on HIGH for 5–5½ minutes, turning over once. If using a microwave burger cooker to cook the burgers individually, read and follow the manufacturer's instructions, particularly for timing. Leave to stand for 2–3 minutes
  Serve in burger buns or pitta bread with salad leaves and a relish of your choice.

COMBINATION MICROWAVE

This recipe is suitable for cooking in a combination microwave. Follow the oven manufacturer's timing guide for good results.

Hot and Sour Pork

Chinese five-spice powder, made from a mixture of ground star anise, Szechuan pepper, cassia, cloves and fennel seed, has a flavour similar to liquorice. If you can't find any, use mixed spice instead.

INGREDIENTS

Serves 4

350g/12oz pork fillet

5ml/1 tsp sunflower oil

2.5cm/1in piece fresh root ginger, grated

1 red chilli, seeded and finely chopped

5ml/1 tsp Chinese five-spice powder

15ml/1 tbsp sherry vinegar

15ml/1 tbsp soy sauce

225g/8oz can pineapple chunks in
natural juice

175ml/6fl oz/³⁄₄ cup chicken stock

20ml/4 tsp cornflour

15ml/1 tbsp water

1 small green pepper, seeded and sliced

115g/4oz baby sweetcorn, halved

salt and ground black pepper

sprig of flat leaf parsley, to garnish

boiled rice, to serve

1 Trim away any visible fat from the pork and cut it into 1cm/¹⁄₂in thick slices.

2 Brush the sunflower oil over the base of a microwaveproof casserole. Microwave on HIGH for 3 minutes, stirring once.

3 Blend the ginger, chilli, five-spice powder, sherry vinegar and soy sauce. Drain the pineapple, reserving the juice. Make the stock up to 300ml/ ¹⁄₂ pint/1¹⁄₄ cups with the juice and mix it with the spices, then pour over the pork.

4 Blend the cornflour with the water and gradually stir it into the pork. Add the vegetables and season to taste.

5 Cover loosely and microwave on HIGH for 14–16 minutes, stirring twice, until the pork and vegetables are almost tender. Stir in the pineapple, cover and microwave on HIGH for 3 minutes, stirring once, until the pineapple is hot and the pork tender. Garnish with flat leaf parsley and serve with rice.

Chow Mein

One of the best known of Chinese dishes, this recipe is easy to prepare and a healthy choice for everyday meals.

Serves 4

225g/8oz dried egg noodles

30ml/2 tbsp oil

1 onion, chopped

1cm/½in piece fresh root ginger, chopped

2 garlic cloves, crushed

30ml/2 tbsp soy sauce

50ml/2fl oz/¼ cup dry white wine

10ml/2 tsp Chinese five-spice powder

450g/1lb/4 cups minced pork

4 spring onions, sliced

50g/2oz oyster mushrooms

75g/3oz canned bamboo shoots, sliced if necessary

15ml/1 tbsp sesame oil

prawn crackers, to serve

1 Place the noodles in a microwaveproof bowl, cover with boiling water, then microwave on HIGH for 4 minutes, stirring once. Drain thoroughly.

2 Place the oil in a large microwaveproof bowl and add the onion, ginger, garlic, soy sauce and wine. Cover and microwave on HIGH for 2–3 minutes, stirring once. Stir in the Chinese five-spice powder.

3 Add the minced pork, cover and microwave on HIGH for 6 minutes, stirring three times to break up the meat during cooking. Mix in the spring onions, mushrooms and bamboo shoots. Cover and microwave on HIGH for 3 minutes, stirring once.

4 Stir in the noodles and sesame oil. Mix all the ingredients together well and serve with prawn crackers.

COOK'S TIP

Lean minced lamb also makes delicious chow mein. Canned bamboo shoots can be replaced by canned water chestnuts for a crunchy texture.

Spiced Chicken with Spinach

A mildly spiced dish using a popular combination of spinach and chicken. This recipe is best made using fresh spinach, but if this is unavailable you can use frozen instead.

INGREDIENTS

Serves 4

225g/8oz fresh spinach leaves, washed but
  not dried

2.5cm/1in piece fresh root ginger, grated

2 garlic cloves, crushed

1 green chilli, roughly chopped

200ml/7fl oz/scant 1 cup water

30ml/2 tbsp oil

2 bay leaves

1.5ml/¼ tsp black peppercorns

1 onion, finely chopped

4 tomatoes, skinned and finely chopped

10ml/2 tsp curry powder

5ml/1 tsp salt

5ml/1 tsp chilli powder

45ml/3 tbsp natural yogurt

8 chicken thighs, skinned

natural yogurt and chilli powder,
  to garnish

masala naan, to serve

1 Place the spinach, without water, in a microwaveproof bowl. Cover and microwave on HIGH for 4 minutes, stirring once. Purée the spinach, ginger, garlic and chilli with 50ml/2fl oz/¼ cup of the water in a food processor or blender.

2 Place the oil in a large microwaveproof dish. Add the bay leaves, black peppercorns and onion, cover and microwave on HIGH for 4 minutes, stirring once.

3 Stir in the tomatoes, curry powder, salt and chilli powder. Cover and microwave on HIGH for 3 minutes, stirring once.

4 Mix in the purée and remaining water. Cover and microwave on HIGH for 2 minutes.

5 Stir in half the yogurt and add the chicken, arranging the pieces in the sauce. Cover and microwave on HIGH for 10 minutes, stirring once.

6 Add the remaining yogurt. Cover and microwave on HIGH for a further 7–8 minutes, or until the chicken is tender. Serve on masala naan, drizzle over some natural yogurt and dust with chilli powder.

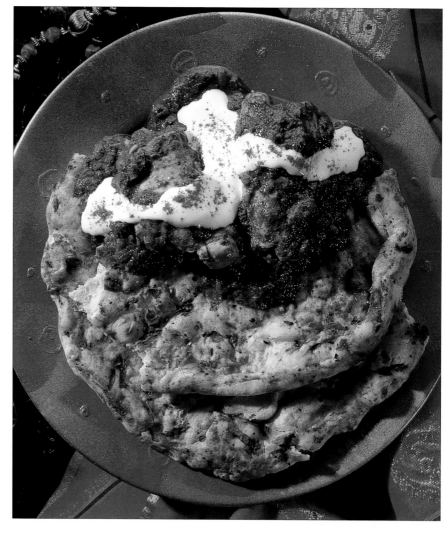

Spicy Lamb Curry

One of the simplest Indian dishes to make, this spicy mixture can be used as a tasty filling for stuffing vegetables, such as peppers and large beefsteak tomatoes.

INGREDIENTS

Serves 4

45ml/3 tbsp oil

1 onion, finely chopped

2 garlic cloves, crushed

2.5cm/1in piece fresh root ginger, grated

2 green chillies, finely chopped

675g/1½lb minced lamb

5ml/1 tsp ground cumin

5ml/1 tsp ground coriander

5ml/1 tsp chilli powder

5ml/1 tsp salt

250ml/8fl oz/1 cup water

175g/6oz frozen peas, thawed

30ml/2 tbsp lemon juice

naan bread and natural yogurt, to serve

1 Place the oil, onion, garlic, ginger and chillies in a large microwaveproof bowl. Cover and microwave on HIGH for 5 minutes, stirring once.

2 Add the minced lamb and stir well to break up the meat. Microwave on HIGH for 5 minutes, stirring once.

3 Stir in the cumin, coriander, chilli powder, salt and water. Cover and microwave on HIGH for 10 minutes, stirring once.

4 Finally, mix in the peas and lemon juice. Microwave on HIGH, uncovered, for 6–8 minutes, or until the meat is tender. Serve with naan bread and natural yogurt.

Chicken Roll

The roll can be prepared and cooked the day before and it will also freeze well. Remove from the fridge about an hour before serving.

INGREDIENTS

Serves 8
1.75kg/4lb chicken

For the stuffing
1 onion, finely chopped
50g/2oz/4 tbsp melted butter
350g/12oz lean minced pork
115g/4oz streaky bacon, chopped
15ml/1 tbsp chopped fresh parsley
10ml/2 tsp chopped fresh thyme
115g/4oz/2 cups fresh white breadcrumbs
30ml/2 tbsp sherry
1 large egg, beaten
25g/1oz/¼ cup shelled pistachio nuts
25g/1oz/¼ cup black olives,
    about 12, stoned
salt and ground black pepper

1 To make the stuffing, place the onion and 25g/1oz/2 tbsp of the butter in a microwaveproof bowl. Cover and microwave on HIGH for 2 minutes, until softened.

2 Turn into a bowl and cool slightly before adding the remaining ingredients. Mix thoroughly and season with salt and ground black pepper.

3 To bone the chicken, use a small, sharp knife to remove the wing tips. Turn the chicken on to its breast and cut a line down the back bone.

4 Cut the flesh away from the carcass, scraping the bones clean. Carefully cut through the sinews around the leg and wing joints and scrape down the bones to free them. Remove the carcass, taking care not to cut through the skin along the breast bone.

5 To stuff the chicken, lay it flat, skin side down and smooth the flesh out as much as possible. Shape the stuffing down the centre of the chicken and fold the sides over the stuffing.

6 Sew the flesh neatly together, using a needle and dark thread. Tie with fine string into a roll. Weigh the stuffed chicken roll. Brush with the remaining butter.

7 Place the roll, with the join underneath, in a roasting bag. Secure with string or an elastic band, making sure there is room for steam to escape. Place in a shallow microwaveproof dish. Microwave on MEDIUM for 9 minutes per 450g/1lb, turning over twice during cooking.

8 Remove the chicken from the bag and brown it under a preheated hot grill, if liked. Leave to cool completely before removing the string and thread. Wrap in foil and chill until ready for serving or freezing.

COMBINATION MICROWAVE

This recipe is suitable for cooking in a combination microwave. Follow the oven manufacturer's timing guide for good results.

COOK'S TIP

Use dark thread for sewing, as it is much easier to see so that you can remove it once the roll is cooked.

Turkish Lamb and Apricot Stew

Cooking this stew on medium power ensures that the lamb is deliciously moist and tender.

INGREDIENTS

Serves 4

1 large aubergine, cubed
30ml/2 tbsp sunflower oil
1 onion, chopped
1 garlic clove, crushed
5ml/1 tsp ground cinnamon
3 whole cloves
450g/1lb boned leg of lamb, cubed
400g/14oz can chopped tomatoes
300ml/½ pint/1¼ cups boiling water
115g/4oz/⅔ cup ready-to-eat dried
   apricots
115g/4oz canned chick-peas, drained
5ml/1 tsp clear honey
salt and ground black pepper
couscous, to serve
30ml/2 tbsp olive oil
30ml/2 tbsp chopped almonds, fried in a
   little oil
chopped fresh parsley

2 Stir in the ground cinnamon and cloves and microwave on HIGH for 30 seconds. Add the lamb and microwave on HIGH for 5 minutes, stirring once.

3 Rinse, drain and pat the aubergine dry, then add to the casserole with the tomatoes, boiling water, apricots and seasoning. Cover and microwave on MEDIUM for 30 minutes, or until the meat is almost tender.

4 Stir in the chick-peas and honey. Cover and microwave on HIGH for 3–5 minutes, or until the lamb is tender. Serve the stew accompanied by couscous with the olive oil, fried almonds and chopped parsley stirred in.

1 Place the aubergine in a colander, sprinkle with salt and leave for 30 minutes. Place the oil in a microwaveproof casserole, add the onion and garlic, cover and microwave on HIGH for 2 minutes, until softened.

Chilli Con Carne

An American recipe that has become a regular feature in many homes. Simple and economical, it is one of the most popular minced beef recipes developed. This recipe isn't highly spiced and so is suitable for young children too.

INGREDIENTS

Serves 4

15ml/1 tbsp oil
225g/8oz/2 cups minced beef
1 onion, quartered
5ml/1 tsp chilli powder
15g/½oz/2 tbsp plain flour
30ml/2 tbsp tomato purée
150ml/¼ pint/⅔ cup beef stock
200g/7oz can chopped tomatoes
200g/7oz can kidney beans, drained
1 green pepper, seeded and chopped
15ml/1 tbsp Worcestershire sauce
75g/3oz/½ cup long grain rice
salt and ground black pepper
soured cream, to serve
chopped fresh parsley, to garnish

1 Place the oil, minced beef, onion and chilli powder in a microwaveproof bowl and microwave on HIGH for 6–8 minutes, stirring twice.

2 Add the flour and tomato purée and microwave on HIGH for 30 seconds, stirring once. Stir in the stock and tomatoes, cover and microwave on HIGH for 12–15 minutes, stirring once.

3 Mix in the kidney beans, chopped green pepper and Worcestershire sauce. Cover and microwave on HIGH for 5–7 minutes, stirring once.

4 Place the rice in a large microwaveproof bowl. Add 250ml/8fl oz/1 cup boiling water and a pinch of salt. Cover loosely and microwave on HIGH for 3 minutes. Stir, re-cover and microwave on MEDIUM for 12 minutes. Leave to stand, covered, for 5 minutes.

5 Fluff up the rice and spoon it on to serving plates. Serve the chilli con carne on the rice. To complete the dish, add a spoonful of soured cream and garnish with fresh parsley.

Pork Crumble

Minced pork combines well with the sweetness of apple and the texture of crunchy vegetables. Served with the satisfying oat topping, this is a meal to tempt all the family.

INGREDIENTS

Serves 4

15ml/1 tbsp oil

1 onion, sliced

450g/1lb/4 cups minced pork

25g/1oz/2 tbsp plain flour

150ml/¼ pint/⅔ cup hot milk

150ml/¼ pint/⅔ cup hot vegetable
  stock

50g/2oz broccoli florets

50g/2oz/½ cup canned sweetcorn,
  drained

1 green eating apple, cored
  and diced

salt and ground black pepper

For the topping

50g/2oz/½ cup instant oatmeal

50g/2oz/½ cup plain flour

15g/½oz/1 tbsp butter

25g/1oz/¼ cup Red Leicester
  cheese, grated

1 Place the oil in a large microwaveproof bowl with the onion. Cover and microwave on HIGH for 2 minutes. Stir in the pork, cover and microwave on HIGH for 4–6 minutes, stirring twice to break up the meat.

2 Stir in the flour, then stir in the milk and stock. Cover and microwave on HIGH for 3 minutes, stirring twice.

3 Mix the broccoli, sweetcorn and apple into the pork mixture and season.

4 Spoon the mixture into four individual microwaveproof dishes that are suitable for grilling.

5 To make the crumble topping, mix the oatmeal and flour, then rub in the butter.

6 Spoon the topping on to the pork mixture and press down with the back of a spoon. Scatter the cheese over the top and microwave on HIGH for 6–8 minutes, repositioning the dishes halfway through cooking. Brown under a preheated hot grill, if liked.

VARIATION

For a rich cheesy topping, mix together crushed potato crisps and grated cheese. Cook as before.

COOK'S TIP

Vary the choice of vegetables according to personal preference. For example, try finely shredded white cabbage instead of the broccoli and/or frozen peas instead of the sweetcorn.

PULSES, PASTA AND GRAINS

~

Chick-pea Curry

Chick-peas are used and cooked in a variety of ways all over India.

INGREDIENTS

Serves 4

225g/8oz/1¼ cups dried chick-peas
50g/2oz tamarind pulp
120ml/4fl oz/½ cup boiling water, plus
   extra for cooking chick-peas
45ml/3 tbsp oil
2.5ml/½ tsp cumin seeds
1 onion, finely chopped
2 garlic cloves, crushed
2.5cm/1in piece fresh root ginger, grated
1 green chilli, seeded and finely chopped
5ml/1 tsp ground cumin
5ml/1 tsp ground coriander
1.5ml/¼ tsp ground turmeric
2.5ml/½ tsp salt
225g/8oz tomatoes, peeled and
   finely chopped
2.5ml/½ tsp garam masala
chopped chillies and onion, to garnish

1 Put the chick-peas in a large bowl and cover with plenty of cold water. Leave to soak overnight.

2 Drain the chick-peas, place in a large microwaveproof bowl and pour in boiling water to cover them. Cover and microwave on HIGH for 10 minutes. Reduce the power setting to MEDIUM and microwave for a further 20–25 minutes, stirring twice and adding extra boiling water to cover the chick-peas, if necessary. Drain thoroughly.

3 Meanwhile, break up the tamarind and soak it in the measured boiling water for about 15 minutes. Rub the resulting tamarind pulp through a sieve into a bowl, discarding any stones and fibre. The tamarind gives the dish a delicious, sharp flavour.

4 Place the oil in a large microwaveproof bowl with the cumin seeds and microwave on HIGH for 1½ minutes. Add the onion, garlic, ginger and chilli, cover and microwave on HIGH for 3 minutes, stirring once.

5 Add the cumin, coriander, turmeric and salt and microwave on HIGH for 1 minute. Stir in the tomatoes and tamarind pulp. Cover and microwave on HIGH for 3 minutes, stirring once.

6 Mix in chick-peas and garam masala. Cover, microwave on HIGH for 6–8 minutes, stir once. Garnish with chillies and onion.

Mung Beans with Potatoes

Mung beans are one of the quicker-cooking pulses that do not require soaking and are therefore very easy to use. In this recipe, they are cooked with potatoes and traditional Indian spices to give a tasty, nutritious dish.

INGREDIENTS

Serves 4

175g/6oz/1 cup mung beans

750ml/1¼ pints/3 cups boiling water

225g/8oz potatoes, cut into
   2cm/¾in chunks

30ml/2 tbsp oil

2.5ml/½ tsp cumin seeds

1 green chilli, seeded and finely chopped

1 garlic clove, crushed

2.5cm/1in piece fresh root ginger,
   finely chopped

1.5ml/¼ tsp ground turmeric

2.5ml/½ tsp chilli powder

5ml/1 tsp salt

5ml/1 tsp sugar

4 curry leaves

5 tomatoes, peeled and finely chopped

15ml/1 tbsp tomato purée

plain rice, to serve

curry leaves, to garnish

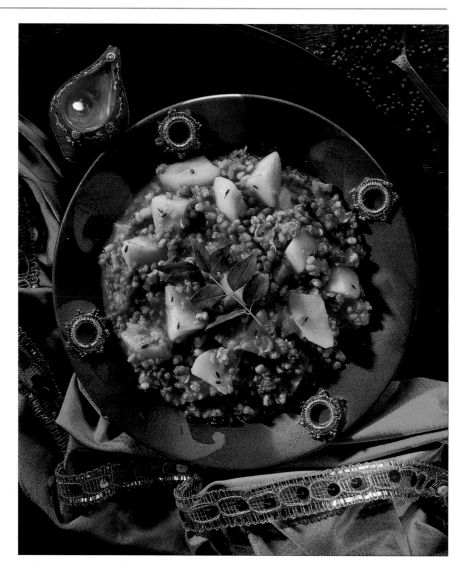

1 Wash the beans and place them in a large microwave-proof bowl with the boiling water and potatoes. Cover and microwave on HIGH for 4 minutes, stirring once. Reduce the power setting to MEDIUM and microwave for a further 12–15 minutes or until the beans are almost tender. Set aside to stand, covered, for 10 minutes.

2 Meanwhile, place the oil and cumin seeds in another large microwaveproof bowl and microwave on HIGH for 1½ minutes. Add the chilli, garlic and ginger, and microwave on HIGH for 2 minutes, stirring once.

3 Add the turmeric, chilli powder, salt and sugar, then microwave on HIGH for 1 minute, stirring once.

4 Stir in the curry leaves, tomatoes and tomato purée. Cover and microwave on HIGH for 3–4 minutes, stirring once, until the sauce thickens slightly. Drain the beans and potatoes, then mix them into the tomato sauce. Serve with plain boiled rice and garnish with curry leaves.

Pasta Bows with Smoked Salmon and Dill

In Italy, pasta cooked with smoked salmon has become very fashionable. This is a quick and quite luxurious sauce.

INGREDIENTS

Serves 4

50g/2oz/4 tbsp butter

6 spring onions, sliced

90ml/6 tbsp dry white wine or vermouth

475ml/16fl oz/2 cups double cream

freshly grated nutmeg

225g/8oz smoked salmon

30ml/2 tbsp chopped fresh dill or 15ml/
   1 tbsp dried dill

freshly squeezed lemon juice

450g/1lb/4 cups pasta bows (farfalle)

salt and ground black pepper

1 While preparing the sauce in the microwave, cook the pasta conventionally in a large saucepan of boiling salted water on the hob according to the packet instructions.

2 Place the butter and spring onions in a microwaveproof bowl. Cover and microwave on HIGH for 1 minute.

3 Add the wine and microwave on HIGH for 2–3 minutes to reduce the liquid to about 30ml/ 2 tbsp. Stir in the cream and add salt, pepper and nutmeg to taste. Microwave on HIGH for 1–2 minutes, stirring twice, until slightly thickened.

4 Cut the smoked salmon into 2.5cm/1in squares and stir into the sauce with the dill. Taste and add a little lemon juice.

5 Drain the pasta well. Toss the pasta with the sauce and serve immediately.

Lemon and Ginger Spicy Beans

A quick meal, made with canned beans. You won't need extra salt as canned beans tend to be salted.

Serves 4

5cm/2in piece fresh ginger root, peeled
   and roughly chopped
3 garlic cloves, roughly chopped
250ml/8fl oz/1 cup cold water
15ml/1 tbsp sunflower oil
1 large onion, thinly sliced
1 fresh red chilli, seeded and
   finely chopped
1.5ml/¼ tsp cayenne pepper
10ml/2 tsp ground cumin
5ml/1 tsp ground coriander
2.5ml/½ tsp ground turmeric
30ml/2 tbsp lemon juice
75g/3oz/⅓ cup chopped fresh
   coriander leaves
400g/14oz can black-eyed beans, drained
   and rinsed
400g/14oz can aduki beans, drained
   and rinsed
400g/14oz can haricot beans, drained
   and rinsed
ground black pepper

3 Add the cayenne pepper, cumin, ground coriander and turmeric, and microwave on HIGH for 1 minute.

4 Stir in the ginger and garlic paste and microwave on HIGH for 1 minute.

5 Stir in the remaining water, lemon juice and fresh coriander. Cover and microwave on HIGH for 4 minutes.

6 Add all the beans to the mixture in the bowl and stir well. Cover and microwave on HIGH for 4–6 minutes, stirring halfway through cooking. Season with pepper and serve.

1 Place the ginger, garlic and 60ml/4 tbsp of the cold water in a blender or food processor and process until smooth.

2 Place the oil in a large microwaveproof bowl with the onion and chilli. Microwave on HIGH for 3 minutes, stirring halfway through cooking.

Rocket, Mangetouts and Pine Nut Pasta

A light but filling pasta dish flavoured with the peppery taste of fresh rocket.

INGREDIENTS

Serves 4

250g/9oz capellini or angel-hair pasta

50g/2oz/¼ cup pine nuts

225g/8oz mangetouts

30ml/2 tbsp water

175g/6oz rocket

30ml/2 tbsp finely grated Parmesan
   cheese (optional)

30ml/2 tbsp olive oil (optional)

1 While preparing the sauce in the microwave, cook the pasta conventionally in a large saucepan of boiling salted water on the hob according to the packet instructions.

2 Place the pine nuts in a microwaveproof dish and microwave on HIGH for 3–5 minutes, stirring every minute, until golden.

3 Carefully top and tail the mangetouts. Place them in a large microwaveproof bowl and add the water. Cover and microwave on HIGH for 2 minutes. Add the rocket and mix lightly.

4 As soon as the pasta is cooked, drain it immediately and toss it with the mangetouts and rocket.

5 Toss the pine nuts into the pasta. Add the Parmesan and olive oil if using. Serve at once.

Tagliatelle with Tomatoes and Courgettes

Serves 3–4

5–6 ripe tomatoes

225g/8oz wholewheat tagliatelle

1.2 litres/2 pints/5 cups boiling water

30ml/2 tbsp olive oil

1 onion, chopped

2 celery sticks, chopped

1 garlic clove, crushed

2 courgettes, sliced

30ml/2 tbsp sun-dried tomato paste

50g/2oz/½ cup flaked almonds, toasted,
   to serve

salt and ground black pepper

1 Place the tomatoes in a bowl and pour in boiling water to cover, then leave to stand for 30 seconds to loosen their skins. Peel, then chop.

2 Place the tagliatelle in a large microwaveproof bowl with the boiling water. Microwave on HIGH for 6 minutes, stirring once. Leave to stand, covered, while cooking the sauce.

3 Place the oil in another microwaveproof bowl and add the onion, celery, garlic and courgettes. Cover and microwave on HIGH for 3–4 minutes, or until the onions are softened.

4 Stir in the tomatoes and sun-dried tomato paste. Microwave on HIGH for 3–4 minutes, then add salt and pepper.

5 Drain the pasta, return it to the bowl and add the sauce. Toss well. Transfer to a serving dish and scatter the toasted almonds over the top to serve.

COOK'S TIP

If using fresh pasta, you'll need double the quantity (450g/1lb) to satisfy 3–4 hearty appetites. Fresh tagliatelle usually only takes 2–3 minutes to cook and is ready when it's tender but still *al dente*, with a bit of bite.

Pasta with Tomato and Smoky Bacon Sauce

*A wonderful sauce to prepare in
mid-summer when the tomatoes are
ripe and sweet.*

INGREDIENTS

Serves 4

900g/2lb ripe tomatoes

450g/1lb/4 cups pasta, any variety

6 rashers smoked streaky bacon

50g/2oz/4 tbsp butter

1 onion, chopped

15ml/1 tbsp chopped fresh oregano or
   5ml/1 tsp dried oregano

salt and ground black pepper

freshly grated Parmesan cheese, to serve

1 Plunge the tomatoes into
boiling water for 1 minute,
then into cold water to stop them
from becoming mushy. Slip off the
skins. Halve the tomatoes, remove
the seeds and cores and roughly
chop the flesh.

2 Cook the pasta in a saucepan
of boiling water according to
the packet instructions. Remove
and discard the rind from the
bacon and chop the rashers.

3 Place the butter in a
microwaveproof bowl and add
the bacon. Microwave on HIGH
for 5 minutes, stirring once, then
add the onion.

4 Microwave on HIGH for a
further 1½ minutes. Add the
tomatoes, seasoning and oregano.
Cover and microwave on HIGH
for 5–6 minutes, stirring twice.

5 Drain the pasta well and toss it
with the sauce. Serve with
grated Parmesan cheese.

Pasta Shells with Smoked Haddock

INGREDIENTS

Serves 4

450g/1lb smoked haddock fillet

1 small leek or onion, thickly sliced

300ml/½ pint/1¼ cups hot skimmed milk

1 bouquet garni (bay leaf, thyme and
 parsley stalks)

25g/1oz low-fat margarine

25g/1oz plain flour

30ml/2 tbsp chopped fresh parsley

225g/8oz pasta shells

salt and ground black pepper

15g/½oz flaked almonds, toasted, to serve

1 While preparing the sauce in the microwave, cook the pasta conventionally in a large saucepan of boiling salted water on the hob according to the packet instructions.

2 Remove all the skin and any bones from the haddock. Arrange the fish fillets in a large microwaveproof dish with the thicker portions to the outside of the dish. Sprinkle with the leek or onion. Add half the milk and the bouquet garni. Cover and microwave on HIGH for 5–6 minutes, rearranging once. Leave to stand for 3 minutes.

3 Strain, reserving the milk for making the sauce, and discard the bouquet garni.

4 Whisk the margarine, flour and remaining milk together in a microwave jug. Microwave on HIGH for 4–6 minutes, whisking every minute, until smooth, boiling and thickened. Season and add the fish and leek or onion.

5 Drain the pasta thoroughly and stir it into the sauce with the chopped parsley. Serve immediately, scattered with toasted flaked almonds.

Turkey Lasagne

This delicious low-fat version of a classic lasagne is very easy to cook in the microwave.

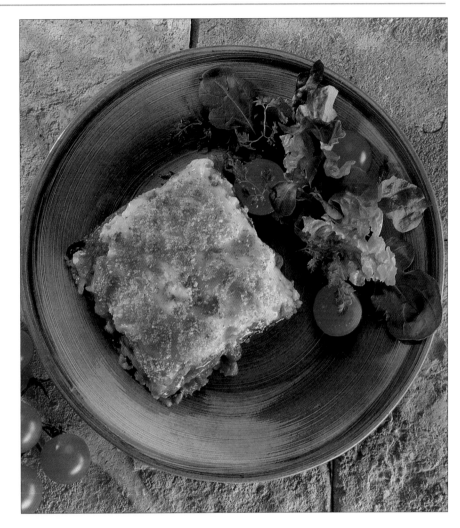

Serves 6–8

1 large onion, chopped

2 garlic cloves, crushed

500g/1¼lb minced turkey meat

450g/1lb carton passata (smooth, thick, sieved tomatoes)

5ml/1 tsp dried mixed herbs

200g/7oz lasagne verdi

900ml/1½ pints/3¾ cups boiling water

225g/8oz frozen leaf spinach, thawed

200g/7oz low-fat cottage cheese

For the sauce

25g/1oz low-fat margarine

25g/1oz plain flour

300ml/½ pint/1¼ cups skimmed milk

1.5ml/¼ tsp ground nutmeg

25g/1oz grated Parmesan cheese

salt and ground black pepper

mixed salad, to serve

1 Mix the onion, garlic and minced turkey in a microwaveproof bowl. Cover and microwave on HIGH for 4 minutes, stirring twice to separate the pieces.

2 Add the passata, herbs and seasoning. Cover and microwave on HIGH for 8 minutes, stirring once.

3 Whisk all the sauce ingredients, except the Parmesan cheese, together in a microwaveproof jug. Microwave on HIGH for 4–6 minutes, whisking every minute, until smooth, boiling and thickened. Adjust the seasoning and stir in the cheese.

4 Place the lasagne in a deep, rectangular microwaveproof dish. Add the boiling water. Cover and microwave on HIGH for 9 minutes. Leave to stand for 15 minutes, then drain well and rinse under cold water. Lay the spinach leaves out on kitchen paper and pat dry.

5 Layer the turkey mixture, prepared lasagne, cottage cheese and spinach in a 2 litre/3½ pint/8 cup microwaveproof dish which is suitable for grilling, starting and ending with a layer of turkey.

6 Spoon the sauce over the top to coat the turkey and microwave on HIGH for 2–3 minutes or until heated through. Brown under a preheated hot grill if liked. Serve with a mixed salad.

COMBINATION MICROWAVE

This recipe is suitable for cooking in a combination microwave. Follow the oven manufacturer's timing guide for good results.

Chicken and Vegetable Risotto

An Italian dish made with short grain arborio rice, which gives this easy one-pot recipe a creamy consistency.

INGREDIENTS

Serves 4

15ml/1 tbsp oil

1 onion, chopped

225g/8oz/2 cups minced chicken

175g/6oz/1½ cups arborio rice

600ml/1 pint/2½ cups boiling
   chicken stock

1 red pepper, seeded and chopped

1 yellow pepper, seeded and chopped

75g/3oz frozen green beans

115g/4oz chestnut mushrooms, sliced

15ml/1 tbsp chopped fresh parsley

salt and ground black pepper

fresh parsley sprigs, to garnish

1 Place the oil, onion and chicken in a large microwave-proof bowl. Cover the bowl and microwave on HIGH for 6–7 minutes, stirring twice.

2 Stir in the rice, stock, red and yellow peppers and green beans. Cover the bowl and microwave on HIGH for 13 minutes, stirring twice.

3 Add the mushrooms and microwave on HIGH for 1 minute. Leave to stand, covered, for 10 minutes.

4 Stir in the chopped parsley and season well to taste. Serve, garnished with parsley sprigs.

VARIATIONS

Make a country-style risotto by using thinly sliced garlic sausage or spicy sausage instead of the chicken and replacing the peppers with shelled broad beans. The green beans can also be replaced with sliced courgettes. To enrich a risotto, use a proportion of dry white wine instead of all chicken stock. For example, try using about a third white wine, making it up to the full quantity with boiling stock. Heat the mixture in the microwave before adding it to the risotto, otherwise the overall cooking time will be longer to allow for the cool liquid.

COOK'S TIP

A traditional risotto has a moist, creamy consistency. Risotto rice, the best being arborio, is short in length but it has the capacity for absorbing a large proportion of liquid during cooking while retaining its shape and some texture. The cooked rice is slightly sticky, so it acts as a type of thickening agent for the excess liquid. In fact, a risotto rice is halfway between familiar long grain rice and traditional pudding rice in terms of cooking quality.

VEGETABLES
AND SALADS

Herby Baked Tomatoes

Dress up sliced, sweet tomatoes with fresh herbs and a crisp topping.

INGREDIENTS

Serves 4-6

675g/1½lb large red and yellow tomatoes
   (about 8)
10ml/2 tsp red wine vinegar
2.5ml/½ tsp wholegrain mustard
1 garlic clove, crushed
10ml/2 tsp water
10ml/2 tsp chopped fresh parsley
10ml/2 tsp snipped fresh chives
25g/1oz/½ cup fine fresh white
   breadcrumbs
salt and ground black pepper
sprigs of flat leaf parsley, to garnish

1 Thickly slice the tomatoes and arrange half of them in a 900ml/1½ pint/3¾ cup microwaveproof dish which is suitable for grilling.

2 Mix the vinegar, mustard, garlic, seasoning and water together. Sprinkle the tomatoes with half the parsley and chives, then drizzle over half the dressing.

3 Lay the remaining tomato slices on top, overlapping them slightly. Drizzle with the remaining dressing. Cover and microwave on HIGH for 6 minutes, rotating the dish twice during cooking.

4 Uncover and sprinkle over the breadcrumbs. Cook under a preheated hot grill until the topping is crisp. Sprinkle with the remaining parsley and chives. Serve immediately, garnished with sprigs of flat leaf parsley.

COMBINATION MICROWAVE

This recipe is suitable for cooking in a combination microwave. Follow the oven manufacturer's timing guide for good results.

Mushroom and Okra Curry

This simple but delicious curry, with its fresh gingery mango relish, is best served with plain basmati rice.

Serves 4

4 garlic cloves, roughly chopped

2.5cm/1in piece fresh ginger root, roughly chopped

1–2 fresh red chillies, seeded and chopped

175ml/6fl oz/¾ cup water

15ml/1 tbsp sunflower oil

5ml/1 tsp coriander seeds

5ml/1 tsp cumin seeds

5ml/1 tsp ground cumin

2 green cardamom pods, seeds removed and ground

pinch of ground turmeric

400g/14oz can chopped tomatoes

450g/1lb mushrooms, quartered if large

225g/8oz okra, trimmed and cut into 1cm/½in slices

30ml/2 tbsp chopped fresh coriander

basmati rice, to serve

For the mango relish

1 large ripe mango, about 500g/1¼lb in weight

1 small garlic clove, crushed

1 onion, finely chopped

10ml/2 tsp grated fresh root ginger

1 fresh red chilli, seeded and finely chopped

pinch each of salt and sugar

1 For the mango relish, peel the mango and cut the flesh from the stone.

2 Mash the mango flesh with a fork or lightly process it in a blender or food processor, and mix in the rest of the relish ingredients. Set the relish aside.

3 Process the garlic, ginger, chillies and 45ml/3 tbsp of the water to a smooth paste in a blender or food processor.

4 Place the sunflower oil in a large microwaveproof bowl. Add the coriander and cumin seeds, and microwave on HIGH for 30 seconds. Add the ground cumin, ground cardamom and turmeric, then microwave on HIGH for a further 30 seconds.

5 Stir in the spice paste, tomatoes, remaining water, mushrooms and okra. Cover and microwave on HIGH for 10–12 minutes, stirring halfway through cooking.

6 Leave to stand, covered, for 5 minutes, until the okra is tender. Stir in the fresh coriander and serve with rice and the mango relish.

COOK'S TIP

When buying okra, look for firm, bright green vegetables that are unblemished. Small to medium okra are best; large pods can be quite tough and coarse, therefore not ideal for microwave cooking. Avoid any that look browned or bruised in places, especially around the stalk end. As with most pre-packed produce, reject sealed packets that look damp inside.

Courgette and Potato Tortilla

INGREDIENTS

Serves 4

30ml/2 tbsp chopped fresh tarragon

4 size 2 eggs, beaten

30ml/2 tbsp olive oil

1 onion, finely chopped

450g/1lb potatoes, diced

1 garlic clove, crushed

2 courgettes, thinly sliced

salt and ground black pepper

1 Stir the tarragon into the eggs and season with salt and pepper. Set aside.

2 Place the oil and onion in a large, shallow microwaveproof dish which is suitable for grilling. Cover and microwave on HIGH for 3 minutes. Add the diced potatoes, garlic and sliced courgettes, cover again and microwave on HIGH for 10 minutes, stirring twice during cooking.

3 Pour the eggs over the vegetables, cover and microwave on HIGH for about 3–5 minutes, rotating the dish twice, until the eggs are beginning to set slightly. Meanwhile, preheat the grill.

4 Place the tortilla under the grill and cook for a few minutes until the top has set and is tinged golden. Cut into wedges and serve from the dish.

COMBINATION MICROWAVE

This recipe is suitable for cooking in a combination microwave. Follow the oven manufacturer's timing guide for good results.

Chicken and Pesto Jackets

Although it is usually served with pasta, pesto also gives a wonderful lift to rice, bread and potato dishes – all good starchy carbohydrates. Here, it is combined with chicken and yogurt to make a low-fat topping for jacket potatoes.

INGREDIENTS

Serves 4

4 baking potatoes, 175g/6oz each, pricked

15ml/1 tbsp pesto

250ml/8fl oz/1 cup low-fat natural yogurt

2 chicken breasts, cooked

1 Arrange the potatoes in a ring pattern on double thick absorbent kitchen paper. Microwave on HIGH for 12–15 minutes, turning over once halfway during cooking. Leave to stand for 3–4 minutes.

2 Stir the pesto into the yogurt until well combined.

COOK'S TIP

The chicken breasts can be cooked in the microwave, if liked. Microwave on HIGH for 3–4 minutes, turning over halfway through cooking.

3 Skin and slice the chicken. Cut the potatoes open and fill with the chicken slices. Top with the pesto-flavoured yogurt and garnish with basil.

Ratatouille

INGREDIENTS

Serves 4

2 large aubergines, roughly chopped

4 courgettes, roughly chopped

150ml/¼ pint/⅔ cup olive oil

2 onions, sliced

2 garlic cloves, chopped

1 large red pepper, seeded and
roughly chopped

2 large yellow peppers, seeded and
roughly chopped

fresh rosemary sprig

fresh thyme sprig

5ml/1 tsp coriander seeds, crushed

3 plum tomatoes, peeled, seeded
and chopped

8 basil leaves, torn

salt and ground black pepper

fresh parsley or basil sprigs, to garnish

1 Sprinkle the aubergines and courgettes with salt, then put them in a colander. Cover with a plate and place a weight on top to press out the bitter juices. Leave for about 30 minutes.

2 Place the olive oil in a large microwaveproof bowl. Add the onions, cover and microwave on HIGH for 5 minutes, until just softened, then add the garlic and microwave on HIGH for a further 1 minute.

3 Rinse the aubergines and courgettes and pat dry with kitchen paper or a dish towel. Stir into the onions with the red and yellow peppers, rosemary, thyme and coriander seeds.

4 Add the tomatoes and season well. Cover and microwave on HIGH for 15–20 minutes, stirring twice during cooking, until the vegetables are soft but not too mushy. Remove the sprigs of herbs. Stir in the torn basil leaves and check the seasoning. Leave to cool slightly and serve warm or cold, garnished with sprigs of parsley or basil.

Mushroom and Fennel Hotpot

Dried shiitake mushrooms add a wonderfully rich flavour to this vegetarian hotpot.

INGREDIENTS

Serves 4

25g/1oz dried shiitake mushrooms

1 small head of fennel or 4 celery sticks

30ml/2 tbsp olive oil

12 shallots, peeled

225g/8oz/2 cups button mushrooms, trimmed and halved

150ml/¼ pint/⅔ cup dry cider

25g/1oz sun-dried tomatoes

30ml/2 tbsp sun-dried tomato paste

1 bay leaf

chopped fresh parsley, to garnish

1 Place the dried shiitake mushrooms in a bowl. Pour over boiling water to cover and set aside for 10 minutes.

2 Roughly chop the fennel or celery sticks. Place the oil in a microwaveproof bowl. Add the shallots and fennel or celery. Cover and microwave on HIGH for 5–6 minutes stirring halfway through cooking. Add the button mushrooms, cover and microwave on HIGH for 1½ minutes.

3 Drain the shiitake mushrooms and reserve the liquid. Cut up any large pieces and add to the fennel or celery.

4 Stir in the cider, sun-dried tomatoes and sun-dried tomato paste. Add the bay leaf. Cover and microwave on HIGH for 2 minutes. Reduce the power setting to MEDIUM and microwave for a further 5–7 minutes, stirring halfway through cooking.

5 Stir in the reserved liquid from the soaked mushrooms. Cover and microwave on MEDIUM for 5–8 minutes until the mixture is very tender. Remove the bay leaf and serve, sprinkled with parsley.

COOK'S TIP

∾

This makes an unusual vegetarian main course or accompaniment. Mushrooms provide useful amounts of vitamins, minerals and fibre.

Courgettes in Citrus Sauce

If baby courgettes are unavailable, use larger ones, but cook them whole. Then halve them lengthways and cut into 10cm/4in lengths.

INGREDIENTS

Serves 4

350g/12oz baby courgettes

30ml/2 tbsp plus 10ml/2 tsp water

4 spring onions, finely sliced

2.5cm/1in piece fresh root ginger, grated

30ml/2 tbsp cider vinegar

15ml/1 tbsp light soy sauce

5ml/1 tsp soft light brown sugar

45ml/3 tbsp vegetable stock

finely grated rind and juice of ½ lemon
   and ½ orange

5ml/1 tsp cornflour

1 Place the courgettes in a microwaveproof bowl with the 30ml/2 tbsp water. Cover and microwave on HIGH for 5 minutes, stirring once or twice during cooking.

2 Meanwhile, put all the remaining ingredients, except the cornflour, into a small microwaveproof jug. Microwave on HIGH for 1½ minutes, stirring halfway through cooking.

3 Blend the cornflour with the 10ml/2 tsp cold water and add to the sauce. Microwave on HIGH for 1 minute, stirring twice, until the sauce has thickened.

4 Pour the sauce over the courgettes and mix gently to coat evenly. Transfer to a warmed serving dish and serve.

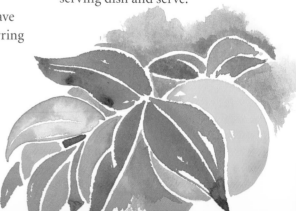

Red Cabbage in Port and Red Wine

A sweet and sour, spicy red cabbage dish, with the added crunch of pears and walnuts.

INGREDIENTS

Serves 6

15ml/1 tbsp walnut oil

1 onion, sliced

2 whole star anise

5ml/1 tsp ground cinnamon

pinch of ground cloves

450g/1lb red cabbage, finely shredded

25g/1oz/2 tbsp dark brown sugar

15ml/1 tbsp red wine vinegar

60ml/4 tbsp red wine

30ml/2 tbsp port

2 pears, cut into 1cm/½in cubes

50g/2oz/¼ cup raisins

salt and ground black pepper

50g/2oz/¼ cup walnut halves

1 Place the oil in a large microwaveproof bowl. Add the onion and microwave on HIGH for 3 minutes, stirring halfway through cooking.

2 Stir in the star anise, cinnamon, cloves and cabbage.

3 Stir in the sugar, vinegar, red wine and port. Cover and microwave on HIGH for 12–15 minutes, stirring twice during cooking, until the cabbage is almost tender.

4 Stir in the pears and raisins. Cover and microwave on HIGH for 5 minutes or until the cabbage and pears are tender. Season to taste, mix in the walnut halves and serve.

Watercress and Potato Salad

New potatoes are equally good hot or cold, and this colourful, nutritious salad is an ideal way of making the most of them.

INGREDIENTS

Serves 4

450g/1lb small new potatoes (unpeeled)

45ml/3 tbsp water

1 bunch watercress

200g/7oz/1½ cups cherry
  tomatoes, halved

30ml/2 tbsp pumpkin seeds

45ml/3 tbsp low-fat fromage frais

15ml/1 tbsp cider vinegar

5ml/1 tsp brown sugar

salt

paprika

3 Place the fromage frais, vinegar, sugar, salt and paprika to taste in a screw-top jar and shake well to mix. Pour over the salad just before serving.

VARIATION

To make Spinach and Potato Salad, substitute about 225g/8oz fresh baby spinach leaves for the watercress.

COOK'S TIP

If you are preparing this salad in advance, mix the dressing in the jar and set aside. Mix the dressing again and toss it into the salad just before serving.

1 Place the potatoes and water in a microwaveproof bowl. Cover and microwave on HIGH for 7–10 minutes, stirring halfway through cooking. Leave to stand, covered, for 3 minutes, then drain and leave to cool.

2 Toss the potatoes, watercress, tomatoes and pumpkin seeds together.

Fruity Brown Rice Salad

An Oriental-style dressing gives this colourful rice salad extra piquancy. Whole grains, like brown rice, are unrefined, so they retain their natural fibre, vitamins and minerals.

INGREDIENTS

Serves 4-6

4 spring onions

115g/4oz/²⁄₃ cup long grain brown rice

300ml/¹⁄₂ pint/1¹⁄₄ cups boiling water

1 small red pepper, seeded and diced

200g/7oz can sweetcorn, drained

45ml/3 tbsp sultanas

225g/8oz can pineapple pieces in
    fruit juice

15ml/1 tbsp light soy sauce

15ml/1 tbsp sunflower oil

15ml/1 tbsp hazelnut oil

1 garlic clove, crushed

5ml/1 tsp finely chopped fresh root ginger

salt and ground black pepper

1 Slice the spring onions at a
slant and set them aside ready
for garnishing the salad.

2 Place the rice in a large
microwaveproof bowl with
the boiling water and a little salt.
Cover loosely and microwave
on HIGH for 3 minutes. Reduce
the power setting to MEDIUM
and microwave for a further
25 minutes, stirring twice
during cooking. Leave to stand,
covered, for 5 minutes.

3 Tip the rice into a serving
bowl and add the red pepper,
sweetcorn and sultanas. Drain the
canned pineapple pieces, reserving
the juice, then toss them lightly
into the rice mixture. Do not
overmix or you will break the
grains of rice.

4 Pour the reserved pineapple
juice into a clean screw-top
jar. Add the soy sauce, sunflower
and hazelnut oils, garlic and
ginger. Add salt and pepper to
taste, then shake well to combine.

5 Pour the dressing over the
salad and toss well. Scatter the
spring onions over the top.

DESSERTS

Sticky Toffee Pudding

INGREDIENTS

Serves 6

115g/4oz/1 cup walnuts, toasted
  and chopped
175g/6oz/³⁄₄ cup butter
175g/6oz/scant 1 cup soft brown sugar
60ml/4 tbsp single cream
30ml/2 tbsp lemon juice
2 eggs, beaten
115g/4oz/1 cup self-raising flour

1 Grease a 900ml/1¹⁄₂ pint microwaveproof pudding basin and add half the walnuts.

2 Mix 50g/2oz/4 tbsp of the butter with 50g/2oz/4 tbsp of the sugar, the cream and 15ml/1 tbsp of the lemon juice in a small microwaveproof bowl. Microwave on HIGH for 1¹⁄₂–2 minutes, stirring once, until smooth. Pour half into the pudding basin, then swirl to coat it a little way up the sides.

3 Beat the remaining butter and sugar until light. Gradually beat in the eggs. Fold in the flour, remaining nuts and lemon juice; spoon into the bowl.

4 Three-quarters cover the basin with clear film and microwave on LOW for 7–10 minutes, until the mixture is well-risen and shrunk away from the sides of the bowl, but still wet on the surface. Leave to stand for 5 minutes.

5 Just before serving, microwave the remaining sauce on HIGH for 1–1¹⁄₂ minutes to reheat. Unmould the pudding on to a warm plate and pour over the warm sauce.

COOK'S TIP

Substitute other nuts of your choice for the walnuts, if wished.

Ruby Plum Mousse

INGREDIENTS

Serves 6

450g/1lb ripe red plums

45ml/3 tbsp granulated sugar

75ml/5 tbsp water

60ml/4 tbsp ruby port

15ml/1 tbsp/1 sachet powdered gelatine

3 eggs, separated

115g/4oz/½ cup caster sugar

150ml/¼ pint/⅔ cup double cream

skinned and chopped pistachio nuts, to
    decorate

crisp biscuits, to serve (optional)

1 Place the plums and granulated sugar in a microwaveproof bowl. Add 30ml/2 tbsp
water. Cover and microwave on
HIGH for 4–5 minutes, stirring
once. Leave to stand for 3 minutes.

2 Press the fruit through a sieve
to remove the stones and
skins. Leave to cool, then stir in the
port.

3 Pour the remaining 45ml/
3 tbsp water into a small bowl,
sprinkle over the gelatine and leave
to soften. Microwave on HIGH for
½–¾ minute until clear and
dissolved. Stir into the plum purée.

4 Whisk the egg yolks and caster
sugar until thick and mousse-
like. Fold in the plum purée. Whip
the cream until it stands in soft
peaks and fold it in gently.

5 Whisk the egg whites until
they hold stiff peaks, then
carefully fold them in using a
metal spoon. Divide among six
glasses and chill until set.

6 Decorate the mousses with
chopped pistachio nuts and
serve with crisp biscuits, if liked.

Warm Autumn Compote

*A simple yet quite sophisticated
dessert using autumnal fruits.*

INGREDIENTS

Serves 4

75g/3oz/6 tbsp caster sugar

1 bottle red wine

1 vanilla pod, split

thinly pared strip of lemon rind

4 pears

2 purple figs, quartered

225g/8oz raspberries

lemon juice, to taste

1 Put the sugar and wine in a
large microwaveproof bowl.
Stir in the vanilla pod and lemon
rind. Microwave on HIGH for 4–6
minutes, stirring three times.

2 Peel and halve the pears, then
scoop out the cores, using a
melon baller. Add the pears to the
syrup and mix well. Cover loosely
and microwave on HIGH for 5–6
minutes, turning over two or three
times during cooking so that they
colour evenly.

3 Add the figs and microwave
on HIGH for a further
2 minutes, until the fruits are tender.

4 Transfer the poached pears
and figs to a serving bowl
using a slotted spoon, then scatter
over the raspberries.

5 Microwave the poaching
liquid, uncovered, on HIGH
for 5–7 minutes to reduce slightly
and concentrate the flavour. Add
a little lemon juice to taste.
Strain the syrup over the fruits
and serve warm.

Hot Bananas with Rum and Raisins

Choose almost-ripe bananas with evenly coloured skins, either all yellow or just green at the tips. Black patches indicate that the fruit is over-ripe.

INGREDIENTS

Serves 4

40g/1½oz/¼ cup seedless raisins

75ml/5 tbsp dark rum

50g/2oz/4 tbsp unsalted butter

60ml/4 tbsp soft light brown sugar

4 ripe bananas, peeled and
   halved lengthways

1.5ml/¼ tsp grated nutmeg

1.5ml/¼ tsp ground cinnamon

30ml/2 tbsp slivered almonds, toasted

chilled cream or vanilla ice cream,
   to serve (optional)

1 Put the raisins in a bowl with the rum. Leave them to soak for about 30 minutes to plump up.

2 Place the butter in a shallow microwaveproof dish and microwave on HIGH for 1 minute or until the butter melts.

3 Stir in the sugar and microwave on HIGH for 1 minute. Add the bananas to the dish and coat them with the sugar mixture, then microwave on HIGH for 4 minutes, turning the fruit over once.

4 Sprinkle the spices over the bananas. Mix the rum and raisins in a small cup.

5 Microwave on HIGH for 30–45 seconds, and then pour them over the bananas. Carefully set alight using a long taper and stir gently to mix.

6 Scatter the slivered almonds over and serve immediately with chilled cream or vanilla ice cream, if you like.

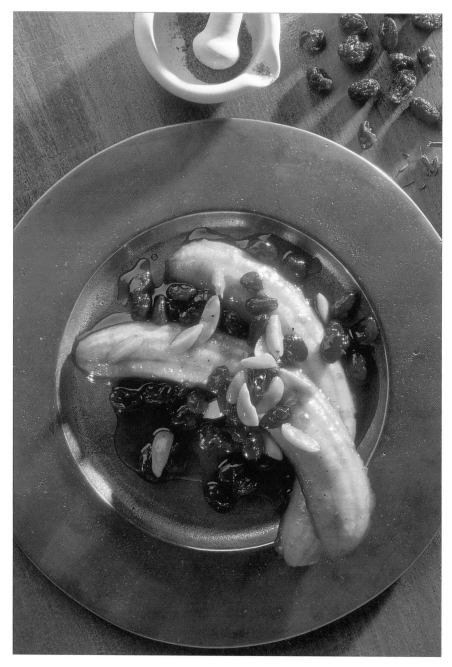

Poached Pears in Red Wine

INGREDIENTS

Serves 4

300ml/¹⁄₂ pint /1¹⁄₄ cups red wine

75g/3oz caster sugar

45ml/3 tbsp honey

juice of ¹⁄₂ lemon

1 cinnamon stick

1 vanilla pod, split open lengthways

5cm/2in thinly pared strip of orange rind

1 clove

1 black peppercorn

4 firm, ripe pears

whipped cream or soured cream, to serve

1 Place the wine, sugar, honey, lemon juice, cinnamon stick, vanilla pod, orange rind, clove and peppercorn in a microwaveproof bowl just large enough to hold the pears standing upright. Microwave on HIGH for 3–5 minutes, until boiling, stirring frequently to dissolve the sugar.

2 Meanwhile, peel the pears, leaving their stems intact. Take a thin slice off the base of each pear so that it will stand neatly square and upright.

3 Place the pears in the wine mixture, spooning it over them. Three-quarters cover the dish with clear film or a lid. Microwave on HIGH for 5–6 minutes until the pears are just tender when pierced with the tip of a knife. Turn and reposition the pears in the bowl two or three times during cooking.

4 Carefully transfer the pears to another bowl using a slotted spoon. Microwave the poaching liquid, uncovered, on HIGH for 15–17 minutes, until the syrup is reduced by half. Leave to cool. Strain the cooled liquid over the pears and chill them for at least 3 hours.

5 Place the pears in individual serving dishes and spoon over a little of the red wine syrup. Serve with whipped or soured cream.

COOK'S TIP

Remember that vanilla pods can be used more than once. Drain and dry a pod thoroughly then store for future use.

Summer Berry Medley

Make the most of glorious seasonal fruits in this refreshing dessert. The sauce is also good swirled into plain or strawberry-flavoured fromage frais or yogurt.

INGREDIENTS

Serves 4-6

175g/6oz redcurrants

175g/6oz raspberries

50g/2oz caster sugar

30–45ml/2–3 tbsp crème de framboise

450–675g/1–1½lb mixed soft summer fruits, such as strawberries, raspberries, blueberries, redcurrants and blackcurrants

vanilla ice cream, to serve

1 Strip the redcurrants from their stalks using a fork and place in a bowl with the raspberries, sugar and crème de framboise. Cover and leave to macerate for 1–2 hours.

2 Put this fruit with its macerating juices in a microwaveproof bowl. Cover and microwave on HIGH for 3 minutes, stirring once, until the fruit is just tender.

3 Pour the fruit into a blender or food processor and blend until smooth. Press through a nylon sieve to remove any pips. Leave to cool, then chill.

4 Divide the mixed soft fruit between four glass serving dishes and pour over the sauce. Serve with scoops of good-quality vanilla ice cream.

Lemon Soufflé with Blackberries

The simple fresh taste of the cold lemon mousse combines well with the rich blackberry sauce, and the colour contrast looks wonderful, too. Blueberries or raspberries make equally delicious alternatives to blackberries.

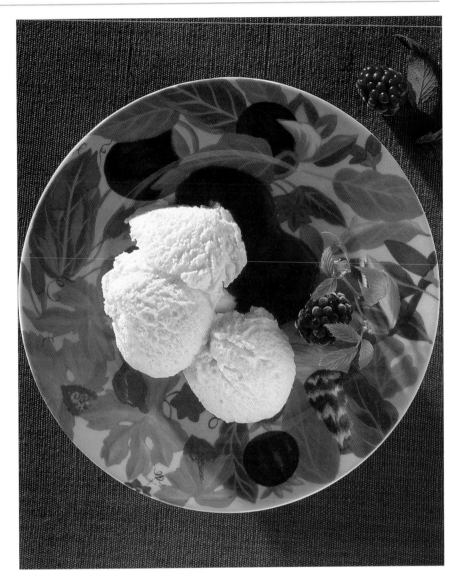

INGREDIENTS

Serves 6

grated rind of 1 lemon and juice
   of 2 lemons
15ml/1 tbsp/1 sachet powdered gelatine
5 x size 4 eggs, separated
150g/5oz/10 tbsp caster sugar
few drops vanilla essence
400ml/14fl oz/1⅔ cups whipping cream
few fresh blackberries and blackberry
   leaves, to decorate

For the sauce
175g/6oz blackberries (fresh or frozen)
30–45ml/2–3 tbsp caster sugar

1 Place the lemon juice in a small microwaveproof bowl, sprinkle over the gelatine and leave to soften. Microwave on HIGH for 30–45 seconds until clear and dissolved. Allow to cool.

2 Put the lemon rind, egg yolks, sugar and vanilla into a large bowl and whisk until the mixture is very thick, pale and creamy.

3 Whisk the egg whites until stiff and almost peaky. Whip the cream until stiff and holding its shape.

4 Stir the gelatine mixture into the yolks, then fold in the whipped cream and lastly the egg whites. When lightly, but thoroughly, blended turn into a 1.5 litre/2½ pint/6¼ cup soufflé dish and freeze for 2 hours.

5 To make the sauce, place the blackberries in a microwaveproof bowl with the sugar. Cover and microwave on HIGH for 2–3 minutes, stirring twice, until the juices begin to run and all the sugar has dissolved. Pass through a sieve to remove the seeds, then chill until ready to serve.

6 When the soufflé is almost frozen, but still spoonable, scoop or spoon out on to individual plates and decorate with blackberries and blackberry leaves. Serve with the blackberry sauce.

Creole Bread and Butter Pudding

INGREDIENTS

Serves 4 – 6

4 ready-to-eat dried apricots, chopped

15ml/1 tbsp raisins

30ml/2 tbsp sultanas

15ml/1 tbsp chopped mixed peel

1 French loaf (about 200g/7oz),
   thinly sliced

50g/2oz/4 tbsp butter, melted

450ml/³⁄₄ pint/1⁷⁄₈ cups milk

150ml/¹⁄₄ pint/²⁄₃ cup double cream

115g/4oz/¹⁄₂ cup caster sugar

3 eggs

2.5ml/¹⁄₂ tsp vanilla essence

30ml/2 tbsp whisky

For the cream

150ml/¹⁄₄ pint/²⁄₃ cup double cream

30ml/2 tbsp Greek-style yogurt

15–30ml/1–2 tbsp whisky

15ml/1 tbsp caster sugar

1 Lightly butter a deep
1.5–1.75 litre/2¹⁄₂–3pint/
6¹⁄₂–7¹⁄₂ cup microwaveproof dish
that is suitable for grilling. Mix the
dried fruits and mixed peel, and
sprinkle a little over the base of the
dish. Brush both sides of the bread
slices with melted butter.

2 Fill the dish with alternate
layers of bread and dried fruit,
finishing with a layer of bread.

3 Pour the milk and cream into
a microwaveproof jug and
microwave on HIGH for 3–4
minutes, or until just boiling.
Meanwhile, whisk the sugar, eggs
and vanilla essence together.

4 Whisk the hot milk and cream
into the eggs and then strain
the mixture over the bread and
fruit. Sprinkle the whisky over the
top. Press the bread into the milk
and egg mixture, cover and leave to
stand for 20 minutes.

5 Microwave on MEDIUM for
10–15 minutes, or until the
mixture is almost set in the
middle, rotating the dish four
times during cooking. Brown
under a preheated hot grill,
if liked.

6 Just before serving, mix the
cream, yogurt, whisky and
sugar into a small microwaveproof
bowl and microwave on HIGH for
1–2 minutes, stirring once. Serve
with the hot pudding.

Chocolate Fudge Sundaes

What better way is there to give everyone a weekend treat than to make these fabulous sundaes for Sunday tea?

Serves 4

4 scoops each vanilla and coffee ice cream

2 small ripe bananas, sliced

whipped cream

toasted flaked almonds

For the sauce

50g/2oz/¼ cup soft light brown sugar

120ml/4fl oz/½ cup golden syrup

45ml/3 tbsp strong black coffee

5ml/1 tsp ground cinnamon

150g/5oz plain chocolate, chopped

85ml/3fl oz/⅓ cup whipping cream

45ml/3 tbsp coffee liqueur (optional)

1 To make the sauce, place the sugar, syrup, coffee and cinnamon in a large microwave-proof jug. Microwave on HIGH for 3–4 minutes, stirring once, until boiling and slightly thickened.

2 Add the chocolate and stir until it has melted. When smooth, stir in the cream and liqueur, if using. Leave the sauce to cool slightly.

3 Fill four serving glasses with a scoop each of vanilla and coffee ice cream.

4 Scatter the sliced bananas over the ice cream. Pour the warm fudge sauce over the bananas, then top each sundae with a generous swirl of whipped cream. Sprinkle with toasted almonds and serve at once before the ice cream melts.

VARIATION

Ring the changes by choosing other flavours of ice cream such as strawberry, toffee or chocolate. In the summer, substitute raspberries or strawberries for the bananas, and scatter chopped roasted hazelnuts on top in place of the flaked almonds.

Apricots with Orange Cream

Mascarpone is a very rich cream cheese made from thick Lombardy cream. It is delicious flavoured with orange as a topping for these chilled, poached apricots.

INGREDIENTS

Serves 4

450g/1lb/2½ cups ready-to-eat dried apricots

thinly pared strip of lemon peel

1 cinnamon stick

45ml/3 tbsp caster sugar

150ml/¼ pint/⅔ cup sweet dessert wine (such as Muscat de Beaumes de Venise)

115g/4oz/½ cup mascarpone cream cheese

45ml/3 tbsp orange juice

pinch of ground cinnamon and fresh mint sprig, to decorate

1 Place the apricots, lemon peel, cinnamon stick and 15ml/ 1 tbsp of the sugar in a pan and cover with 450ml/¾ pint/1⅞ cups cold water. Cover loosely and microwave on HIGH for 10 minutes. Leave to stand for about 5 minutes, then microwave on MEDIUM for 5–8 minutes until the fruit is tender.

2 Stir in the dessert wine. Leave until cold, then chill for 3–4 hours or overnight.

3 Mix together the mascarpone cheese, orange juice and remaining sugar in a bowl and beat well until smooth. Chill until required.

4 Just before serving, remove the cinnamon stick and lemon peel from the apricots. Serve with a spoonful of the chilled mascarpone orange cream, sprinkled with a little cinnamon and decorated with a sprig of fresh mint.

Rhubarb and Orange Fool

Perhaps this traditional English pudding got its name because it is so easy to make that even a 'fool' can attempt it.

INGREDIENTS

Serves 4

30ml/2 tbsp orange juice

5ml/1 tsp finely shredded orange rind

1kg/2¼ lb (about 10–12 stems) rhubarb, chopped

15ml/1 tbsp redcurrant jelly

45ml/3 tbsp caster sugar

150g/5oz prepared thick, creamy custard

150ml/¼ pint/⅔ cup double cream, whipped

sweet biscuits, to serve

1 Place the orange juice and rind, the rhubarb, redcurrant jelly and sugar in a microwave-proof bowl. Cover and microwave on HIGH for 8–10 minutes, stirring once, until the rhubarb is just tender but not mushy. Leave to cool completely.

2 Drain the cooled rhubarb to remove some of the liquid and reserve a few pieces with a little orange rind for decoration. Purée the remaining rhubarb in a food processor or blender, or press it through a sieve.

3 Stir the custard into the purée, then fold in the whipped cream. Spoon the fool into individual bowls, cover and chill. Just before serving, top with the reserved fruit and rind. Serve with crisp, sweet biscuits.

Fruit and Rice Ring

This unusual rice pudding looks beautiful turned out of a ring mould, but if you prefer, stir the fruit into the rice and serve it in individual dishes.

INGREDIENTS

Serves 4

65g/2½oz/5 tbsp short grain rice

900ml/1½ pints/3¾ cups semi-skimmed
   milk

1 cinnamon stick

45ml/3 tbsp sugar

finely grated rind of 1 small orange

175g/6oz/1½ cups mixed dried fruit

175ml/6fl oz/¾ cup orange juice

1 Place the rice, milk and cinnamon stick in a large microwaveproof bowl. Cover and microwave on HIGH for 6–8 minutes, stirring two or three times, until boiling. Reduce the power setting to MEDIUM and microwave for a further 30 minutes, stirring twice, until no liquid remains. Remove the cinnamon stick and stir in the sugar and orange rind.

2 Place the fruit and orange juice in another microwave-proof bowl. Cover and microwave on HIGH for 6 minutes, then reduce the power setting to MEDIUM and microwave for 10–15 minutes, until tender and no liquid remains.

3 Tip the fruit into the base of a lightly oiled 1.5 litre/2½ pint/ 6¼ cup ring mould. Spoon the rice over, smoothing it down firmly and chill the pudding.

4 To serve the ring, run a knife around the edge of the mould and turn out the rice carefully on to a serving plate.

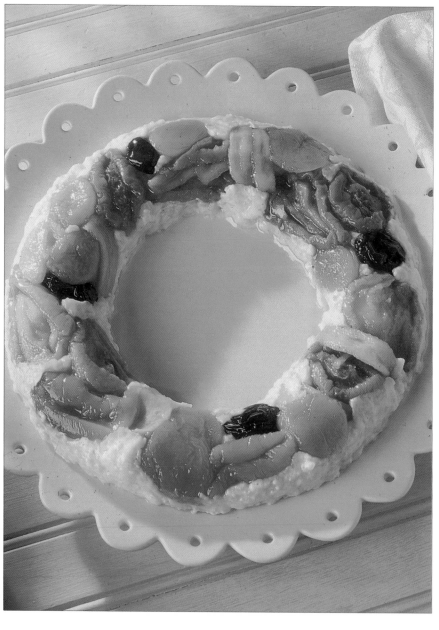

Castle Puddings with Custard

INGREDIENTS

Serves 4–8

about 45ml/3 tbsp blackcurrant, straw-
    berry or raspberry jam
115g/4oz/½ cup butter
115g/4oz/generous ½ cup caster sugar
2 eggs, beaten
few drops of vanilla essence
130g/3½oz/generous cup self-raising flour

For the custard
450ml/¾ pint/scant 2 cups milk
4 eggs
25–30ml/1½–2 tbsp sugar
few drops of vanilla essence

1 Butter eight microwaveproof individual pudding bowls or large teacups and put about 10ml/2 tsp of the jam in the base.

2 Cream the butter and sugar together in a bowl until light and fluffy, then gradually beat in the eggs, beating well after each addition and adding the vanilla essence towards the end. Fold in the flour, then divide the mixture between the bowls or cups.

3 Microwave on HIGH for 3–4 minutes, or until just set. Allow to stand for 3 minutes, then turn each out on to a warmed serving plate. Keep warm.

4 To make the custard, place the milk in a microwaveproof jug and microwave on HIGH for 4 minutes. Beat the eggs and sugar in a microwaveproof bowl, then gradually whisk in the hot milk.

5 Reduce the power setting to MEDIUM HIGH and microwave for 5–6 minutes, stirring every 1 minute until the custard is thick enough to coat the back of a spoon. Do not allow to boil. Stir in the vanilla essence. Serve with the warm puddings.

BAKING

Feta Cheese and Chive Scones

INGREDIENTS

Makes 9

115g/4oz/1 cup self-raising flour

150g/5oz/1¼ cups self-raising wholemeal
flour

2.5ml/½ tsp salt

75g/3oz feta cheese

15ml/1 tbsp snipped fresh chives

150ml/¼ pint/⅔ cup skimmed milk, plus
extra for glazing

1.5ml/¼ tsp cayenne pepper

1 Sift the flours and salt into a
mixing bowl, adding any bran
left over from the flour in the sieve.

2 Crumble the feta cheese and
rub into the dry ingredients.
Stir in the chives, then add the
milk and mix to a soft dough.

3 Turn out the dough on to a
floured surface and lightly
knead until smooth. Roll out to
2cm/¾in thick and stamp out nine
scones with a 6cm/2½in biscuit
cutter. Brush with skimmed milk,
then sprinkle over the cayenne
pepper. Place the scones on a
piece of non-stick parchment in
the microwave, spacing them
well apart.

4 Microwave on HIGH for
3–3½ minutes, repositioning
the scones twice during cooking.
Insert a skewer into the centre of
each scone; if it comes out clean,
the scone is cooked. Return any
uncooked scones to the microwave
and microwave for a further 30
seconds. Brown under a preheated
hot grill until golden, if liked.

Carrot and Pecan Cake

Fructose is used as the sweetening agent in this recipe. It has one and a half times the sweetening power as the same weight of sugar, but only has the same number of calories.

INGREDIENTS

Serves 6–8

175g/6oz/1¼ cups carrots, grated
90ml/3fl oz/⅓ cup sunflower oil
30ml/2 tbsp milk
2 eggs, beaten
75g/3oz/6 tbsp fructose
75g/3oz/⅔ cup plain flour
5ml/1 tsp baking powder
5ml/1 tsp bicarbonate of soda
10ml/2 tsp ground cinnamon
75g/3oz/½ cup raisins
25g/1oz/¼ cup shelled pecans, chopped
icing sugar, to dust

1 Grease an 18cm/7in microwaveproof round cake dish and line it with greaseproof paper.

2 In a large bowl, mix the carrots with the oil, milk, eggs and fructose, beating well.

3 Sift in the flour with the baking powder, bicarbonate of soda and cinnamon. Fold the dry mixture into the egg mixture, then stir in the raisins and pecans. Spoon into the prepared cake dish and level the surface.

4 Place the cake dish on an inverted saucer in the microwave. Microwave on MEDIUM for 9 minutes, giving the dish a quarter turn every 3 minutes. Increase the power setting to HIGH and microwave for a further 2–3 minutes, giving the dish a quarter turn after 1½ minutes.

5 The cake is cooked when it shrinks from the sides of the dish. Leave the cake to stand for 10 minutes before turning it out of the dish to cool on a wire rack.

6 Sprinkle with sifted icing sugar to serve.

Apple and Hazelnut Shortcake

INGREDIENTS

Serves 8–10

150g/5oz/1 cup wholemeal flour

50g/2oz/4 tbsp ground hazelnuts

50g/2oz/4 tbsp icing sugar, sifted

150g/5oz/10 tbsp unsalted butter or
   margarine

3 sharp eating apples

5ml/1 tsp lemon juice

15-30ml/1-2 tbsp caster sugar, or to taste

15ml/1 tbsp chopped fresh mint or 5ml/
   1 tsp dried mint

250ml/8fl oz/1 cup whipping cream or
   crème fraîche

few drops vanilla essence

few mint leaves and whole hazelnuts,
   to decorate

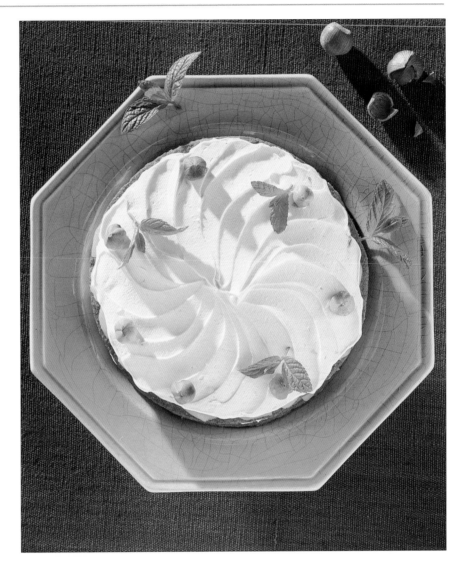

1 Process the flour, ground hazelnuts and icing sugar with the butter in a food processor in short bursts. Alternatively, rub the butter into the dry ingredients until they come together. Do not overwork the mixture. Bring the dough together, adding a very little iced water, if necessary. Knead briefly, wrap in greaseproof paper and chill for 30 minutes.

2 Line the base of a 23cm/9in round shallow microwave-proof dish with greaseproof paper. Roll out the shortcake mixture on a lightly floured surface to a round measuring about 23cm/9in in diameter.

3 Lift into the dish and press down well with the back of a spoon to level the surface and sides. Microwave on LOW for 8 minutes or until a skewer, inserted into the centre of the shortcake, comes out clean. Give the dish a quarter-turn every 2 minutes during cooking. Brown under a preheated hot grill until golden, if liked. Allow to cool.

4 Meanwhile, peel, core and chop the apples. Place in a microwaveproof bowl with the lemon juice. Add sugar to taste, cover and microwave on HIGH for 5–7 minutes, stirring once, until tender. Mash the apple gently with the chopped fresh mint and leave to cool.

5 Whip the cream with the vanilla essence. Place the shortcake on a serving plate and top with the cooked apple.

6 Top the shortcake with the cream, swirling it into a decorative pattern. Decorate with a few mint leaves and whole hazelnuts. Serve at once.

COMBINATION MICROWAVE

This recipe is suitable for cooking in a combination microwave. Follow the oven manufacturer's timing guide for good results.

Strawberry and Hazelnut Roulade

INGREDIENTS

Serves 6–8

2 large eggs

50g/2oz/¼ cup caster sugar

50g/2oz/½ cup plain flour, sifted twice

40g/1½oz shelled hazelnuts, ground

120ml/4fl oz/½ cup double cream

1 egg white

175g/6oz/1½ cups strawberries, sliced

1 Line a 28 x 18cm/11 x 7in shallow rectangular microwaveproof dish with lightly oiled greaseproof paper, leaving about 5cm/2in of paper overlapping at the edges.

2 Whisk the eggs and caster sugar in a bowl until the mixture is very thick and has trebled in volume. Sift the flour over the egg mixture and fold it in with a metal spoon. Pour the mixture in the prepared dish, spreading it evenly.

3 Microwave on HIGH for 2½–3 minutes, until it is just firm in the centre, giving the dish a half turn once during the cooking time. Leave to stand for 3 minutes.

4 Sprinkle a sheet of greaseproof paper with the ground hazelnuts. Turn the sponge out on to the hazelnuts. Remove the lining paper. Hold another piece of greaseproof paper under a tap for a few seconds to dampen it; crumple it up, spread it out again and lay it on top of the cooked sponge. Roll the cake up from one of the shorter edges, enclosing the paper. Let the cake cool completely on a wire rack.

5 Meanwhile, whip the cream until it stands in soft peaks. In another bowl, beat the egg white until stiff and fold into the cream, mixing well.

6 Unroll the sponge, remove the paper, spread the cream over the surface and dot with the sliced strawberries. Roll up the cake again and place on a serving plate, seam side down. Chill the roulade for at least 1 hour, until it becomes firm enough to slice. Just before serving, trim the ends to neaten.

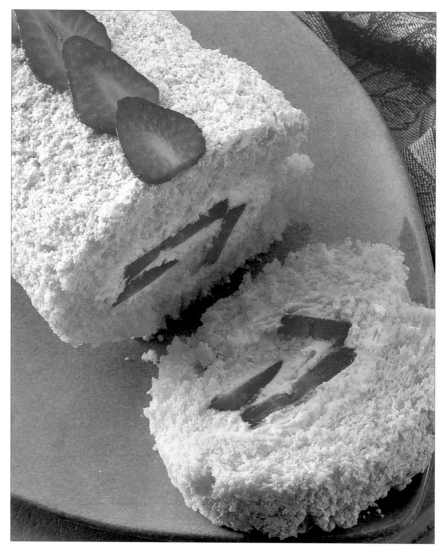

Boston Banoffee Pie

INGREDIENTS

Makes a 20cm/8in pie

225g/8oz/1 cup butter

150g/5oz/1¼ cups plain flour

50g/2oz/4 tbsp caster sugar

200g/7oz can skimmed, sweetened
   condensed milk

115g/4oz/⅔ cup soft light brown sugar

30ml/2 tbsp golden syrup

2 small bananas, sliced

a little lemon juice

whipped cream, to decorate

5ml/1 tsp grated plain chocolate

1 Rub 115g/4oz/½ cup of the butter into the flour. Alternatively, process in a food processor until crumbled. Stir in the caster sugar.

2 Squeeze the mixture together with your hands until it forms a dough. Press into the base of a 20cm/8in microwaveproof flan dish. Cut the pastry away, leaving a 5mm/¼in overlap above the dish to allow for any shrinkage. Prick the base and sides well with a fork.

3 Place a double-thick layer of absorbent kitchen paper over the base, easing it into position around the edges. Microwave on HIGH for 3½ minutes, giving the dish a quarter turn every minute. Remove the paper and microwave on HIGH for a further 1½ minutes. Allow to cool.

4 Place the remaining 115g/4oz/½ cup butter in a large microwaveproof bowl or jug with the condensed milk, brown sugar and golden syrup. Microwave on HIGH for 3 minutes, mixing well twice during cooking.

5 Microwave on HIGH for a further 3–5 minutes, until the mixture thickens and turns a light caramel colour, stirring three times. Pour into the cooked pastry base and leave until cold.

6 Sprinkle the bananas with lemon juice and arrange on top of the caramel filling. Pipe a swirl of whipped cream in the centre and sprinkle with the grated chocolate.

Spiced Banana Muffins

Wholemeal muffins, with banana for added fibre, make a delicious, healthy treat at any time of the day. If liked, slice off the tops and fill with a teaspoon of jam or marmalade.

INGREDIENTS

Makes 12

75g/3oz/³⁄₄ cup wholemeal flour

50g/2oz/¹⁄₂ cup plain flour

10ml/2 tsp baking powder

pinch of salt

5ml/1 tsp mixed spice

40g/1¹⁄₂oz/¹⁄₄ cup soft light brown sugar

50g/2oz/1/4 cup soft margarine

1 egg, beaten

150ml/¹⁄₄ pint/²⁄₃ cup semi-skimmed milk

grated rind of 1 orange

1 ripe banana

20g/³⁄₄oz/¹⁄₄ cup porridge oats

20g/³⁄₄oz/scant ¹⁄₄ cup chopped hazelnuts

1 Sift together both flours, the baking powder, salt and mixed spice into a bowl, then tip the bran remaining in the sieve into the bowl. Stir in the sugar.

2 Place the margarine in a microwaveproof bowl and microwave on HIGH for 1 minute, until melted. Cool the margarine slightly, then beat in the egg, milk and grated orange rind.

3 Gently fold in the dry ingredients. Mash the banana with a fork, then stir it gently into the mixture, being careful not to overmix.

4 Use the mixture to half-fill twelve double-thick bun cases. Cook six at a time, by placing them in a microwave muffin tray or in ramekin dishes. Combine the oats and hazelnuts and sprinkle a little of the mixture over each muffin.

5 Place in the microwave, arranging the dishes in a ring pattern. Microwave on HIGH for 2¹⁄₂–3 minutes, rearranging once during cooking. Repeat with the remaining six muffins. Transfer to a wire rack and remove from their paper cases when cool enough to handle. Serve warm or cold.

Courgette and Walnut Loaf

Cardamom seeds impart their distinctive aroma to this loaf. Serve spread with ricotta and honey for a delicious snack.

INGREDIENTS

Makes 1 loaf

3 eggs

75g/3oz/⅓ cup light muscovado sugar

120ml/4fl oz/½ cup sunflower oil

225g/8oz/2 cups wholemeal flour

5ml/1 tsp baking powder

5ml/1 tsp bicarbonate of soda

5ml/1 tsp ground cinnamon

3ml/¾ tsp ground allspice

7.5ml/1½ tsp green cardamoms, seeds removed and crushed

150g/5oz courgette, coarsely grated

115g/4oz/½ cup walnuts, chopped

50g/2oz/¼ cup sunflower seeds

1 Line the base and sides of a 900g/2lb loaf dish with non-stick baking paper.

2 Beat the eggs and sugar together in a large bowl and gradually add the oil.

3 Sift the flour into a separate bowl, adding the baking powder, bicarbonate of soda, cinnamon and allspice.

4 Mix the dry ingredients into the egg mixture, adding the cardamoms, courgette and walnuts. Reserve 15ml/1 tbsp of the sunflower seeds, then add the remainder to the mixture.

5 Spoon the mixture into the loaf dish, level the top and sprinkle with the reserved sunflower seeds.

6 Shield each end of the dish with a smooth piece of foil, shiny side in. Cover with clear film and microwave on HIGH for 8–9 minutes, giving the dish a quarter turn three or four times.

7 Remove the clear film and foil for the last 1½ minutes, until the loaf is cooked, when a skewer inserted in the centre comes out clean. Allow to cool for 5 minutes before turning out on to a rack to cool. Brown under a preheated hot grill before serving, if liked.

COMBINATION MICROWAVE

This recipe is suitable for cooking in a combination microwave. Follow the oven manufacturer's timing guide for good results.

Kugelhopf

INGREDIENTS

Serves 10–12

50g/2oz/1 cup digestive biscuits, crushed

15 blanched almonds

300ml/½ pint/1¼ cups milk

25g/1oz fresh yeast or 15g/½oz dried yeast

25g/1oz/2 tbsp caster sugar

450g/1lb/4 cups plain flour

175g/6oz/10 tbsp butter or margarine

3 large eggs, beaten

2.5ml/½ tsp salt

75g/3oz/½ cup sultanas

50g/2oz/⅓ cup raisins

25g/1oz/2 tbsp currants

grated rind of 1 lemon

icing sugar, to dust

strawberries, to serve

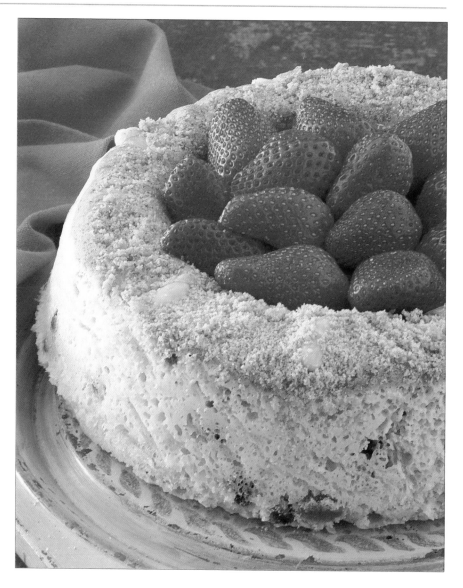

1 Grease a 23cm/9in diameter microwaveproof ring mould and sprinkle the mould with the digestive biscuit crumbs. Arrange the almonds on the base.

2 Pour the milk into a jug and microwave on HIGH for 1 minute or until tepid. Stir in the fresh yeast; or reconstitute the dried yeast with the milk according to the packet instructions, adding 5ml/1 tsp of the caster sugar.

3 Place 175g/6oz/1½ cups of the flour in a microwaveproof bowl and gradually beat in the yeast mixture.

4 Cover loosely with clear film and microwave on DEFROST for 1½–2 minutes. Leave to stand until well risen and frothy, about 10–15 minutes.

5 Place the butter or margarine in a microwaveproof bowl and microwave on HIGH for 1–1½ minutes to melt. Add to the risen batter, together with the remaining sugar and flour, the eggs and salt. Beat the mixture well with a wooden spoon. Stir in the sultanas, raisins, currants and lemon rind, mixing well. Spoon into the prepared mould and smooth the surface with a knife.

6 Cover the batter loosely with clear film and microwave on DEFROST for 8–9 minutes, or until the batter has risen to the top of the mould. Leave to stand for 10 minutes, then microwave, uncovered, on HIGH for 6 minutes, giving the dish a quarter turn three times during cooking. Leave to stand for 5 minutes before turning out onto a wire rack.

7 When cool, dust the top with icing sugar and fill the centre with strawberries before serving.

Chocolate and Orange Angel Cake

This light-as-air sponge with its fluffy icing is virtually fat free, yet tastes heavenly. Make the icing conventionally on the hob for best results.

INGREDIENTS

Serves 10

25g/1oz/¼ cup plain flour

15g/½oz/2 tbsp reduced-fat cocoa powder

15g/½oz/2 tbsp cornflour

pinch of salt

5 egg whites

2.5ml/½ tsp cream of tartar

115g/4oz/scant ½ cup caster sugar

blanched and shredded rind of 1 orange, to decorate

For the icing

200g/7oz/1 cup caster sugar

75ml/5 tbsp water

1 egg white

1 Sift the flour, cocoa powder, cornflour and salt together three times. Lightly whisk the egg whites in a large bowl until foamy. Add the cream of tartar, then whisk until soft peaks form.

2 Add the caster sugar to the egg whites a spoonful at a time, whisking after each addition. Sift a third of the flour and cocoa mixture over the meringue and gently fold in. Repeat, sifting and folding in the flour and cocoa mixture twice more.

3 Spoon the mixture into a microwaveproof 20cm/8in ring mould and level the top. Microwave on MEDIUM for 10–12 minutes, rotating the dish twice. Leave to stand for 5–10 minutes. Turn upside-down on a wire rack and leave to cool in the dish. Carefully ease out of the dish.

4 Make the icing conventionally: put the sugar in a saucepan with the water and stir over low heat until dissolved. Boil until the syrup reaches a temperature of 120°C/240°F on a sugar thermometer or when a drop of the syrup forms a soft ball when dropped into a cup of cold water. Remove from the heat.

5 Whisk the egg white until stiff. Add the syrup in a thin stream, whisking all the time. Continue to whisk until the mixture is very thick and fluffy.

6 Spread the icing over the top and sides of the cooled cake. Sprinkle the orange rind over the top of the cake and serve.

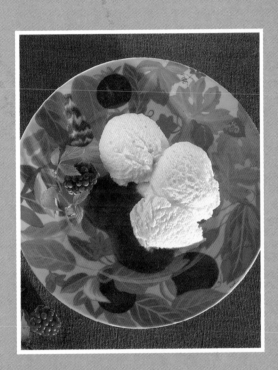

Cooking and Defrosting Charts

~

Cooking Fish and Shellfish

COD steamed steaks and fillets	450g/1lb fillets 2 x 225g/8oz steaks 4 x 225g/8oz steaks	HIGH	Arrange fish fillets in a microwaveproof dish so that the thinner tail ends are to the centre. Fold in any flaps of skin on steaks and secure with wooden cocktail sticks. Dot with a little butter, sprinkle with seasoning and add a dash of lemon juice. Cover and microwave for 5–7 minutes for 450g/1lb fillets; 5 minutes for 2 x 225g/8oz steaks; and 8–9 minutes for 4 x 225g/8oz steaks, rearranging once halfway through cooking. Leave to stand, covered, for 3 minutes before serving.
FISH CAKES 	4 x 75g/3oz	HIGH	Place in a shallow microwaveproof dish and brush with a little melted butter if liked. Microwave for 5 minutes, turning over once, halfway through cooking. Times refer to chilled or fresh fish cakes (thaw frozen fish cakes before cooking). Leave to stand for 2–3 minutes before serving. If liked, the fish cakes can be cooked in a preheated browning dish.
FISH FINGERS 	2 4 6 8 12	HIGH	For best results cook in a preheated browning dish. Microwave for 1½ minutes for 2; 2 minutes for 4; 3 minutes for 6; 4 minutes for 8; and 5 minutes for 12 fish fingers, turning over once, halfway through cooking. Times refer to frozen fish fingers. Leave to stand for 1–2 minutes before serving.
FISH ROES 	115g/4oz 225g/8oz	LOW	Rinse the fish roes and place in a microwaveproof dish with a large knob of butter and seasoning to taste. Cover and microwave for 4–4½ minutes for 115g/4oz; and 6–8 minutes for 225g/8oz fish roes, stirring once halfway through cooking. Leave to stand, covered, for 2 minutes before serving.
HADDOCK steamed steaks and fillets	450g/1lb fillets 2 x 225g/8oz steaks 4 x 225g/8oz steaks	HIGH	Arrange the fish fillets in a microwaveproof dish so that the thinner tail ends are to the centre. Fold in any flaps of skin on steaks and secure with wooden cocktail sticks. Dot with a little butter, sprinkle with seasoning and add a dash of lemon juice. Cover and microwave for 5–7 minutes for 450g/1lb fillets; 5 minutes for 2 x 225g/8oz steaks; and 8–9 minutes for 4 x 225g/8oz steaks, rearranging once halfway through cooking. Leave to stand, covered, for 3 minutes before serving.
HALIBUT steaks	2 x 225g/8oz steaks	HIGH	Fold in any flaps of skin and secure with wooden cocktail sticks. Place in a shallow microwaveproof dish and dot with a little butter. Season with salt, pepper and lemon juice. Cover and microwave for 4–5 minutes. Leave to stand, covered, for 2–3 minutes before serving.
HERRING fresh whole	per 450g/1lb	HIGH	Remove heads and clean and gut before cooking. Slash the skin in several places to prevent bursting during cooking. Place in a shallow microwaveproof dish and season to taste. Shield the tail ends of the fish if liked. Cover with greaseproof paper and microwave for 3–4 minutes per 450g/1lb, turning over once halfway through cooking. Leave to stand, covered, for 2–3 minutes before serving.
KIPPERS fillets	2 4 8	HIGH	If buying whole fish then remove heads and tails. Place skin-side down in a shallow microwaveproof cooking dish. Cover loosely and microwave for 1–2 minutes for 2 fillets; 3–4 minutes for 4 fillets; and 6–7 minutes for 8 fillets, rearranging once halfway through cooking. Leave to stand, covered, for 2–3 minutes before serving.
LOBSTER to reheat cooked whole lobster and tails	450g/1lb whole 450g/1lb tails	HIGH	Place in a shallow microwaveproof dish and cover loosely. Microwave for 6–8 minutes for 450g/1lb whole; and 5–6 minutes for 450g/1lb tails, turning over once halfway through cooking. Leave to stand, covered, for 5 minutes before serving.

MACKEREL fresh whole	per 450g/1lb	HIGH	Remove heads and clean and gut before cooking. Slash the skin in several places to prevent bursting during cooking. Place in a shallow microwave-proof dish and season to taste. Shield the tail ends of the fish if liked. Cover with greaseproof paper and microwave for 3–4 minutes per 450g/1lb, turning over once halfway through cooking. Leave to stand, covered, for 2–3 minutes before serving.
MUSSELS fresh steamed	675g/1½lb	HIGH	Sort the mussels and scrub thoroughly with cold running water. Place in a microwaveproof dish with 75ml/5 tbsp water, fish stock or dry white wine. Cover loosely and microwave for 5 minutes, stirring once halfway through cooking. Remove with a slotted spoon, discarding any mussels that do not open. Thicken the cooking juices with a little beurre manié, (butter and flour paste), if liked, to serve with the mussels.
PLAICE steamed fillets	450g/1lb fillets	HIGH	Arrange fish fillets in a microwaveproof dish so that the thinner tail ends are to the centre of the dish. Dot with a little butter, sprinkle with seasoning and add a dash of lemon juice. Cover and microwave for 4–6 minutes, rearranging once halfway through cooking. Leave to stand, covered, for 3 minutes before serving.
RED OR GREY MULLET fresh whole	2 x 250g/9oz 4 x 250g/9oz	HIGH	Clean and gut before cooking. Place in a shallow microwaveproof dish and slash the skin in several places to prevent bursting during cooking. Cover and microwave for 4–5 minutes for 2 x 250g/9oz mullet; and 8–9 minutes for 4 x 250g/9oz mullet, turning over once halfway through cooking. Leave to stand, covered, for 5 minutes before serving.
SALMON steamed steaks	2 x 225g/8oz 4 x 225g/8oz	HIGH	Place in a shallow microwaveproof dish so that the narrow ends are to the centre of the dish. Dot with butter and sprinkle with lemon juice and salt and pepper. Cover with greaseproof paper and microwave for 2½–3 minutes for 2 x 225g/8oz steaks; and 4½–5¾ minutes for 4 x 225g/8oz steaks, turning over once halfway through cooking. Leave to stand, covered, for 5 minutes before serving.
	4 x 175g/6oz steaks	MEDIUM	Prepare and cook as above but use MEDIUM power and allow 10½–11½ minutes.
whole salmon and salmon trout	450g/1lb 900g/2lb 1.5kg/3–3½lb 1.75kg/4–4½lb	HIGH	Remove the head if liked. Slash or prick the skin in several places to prevent bursting during cooking. Place in a microwaveproof dish with 150ml/¼ pint/⅔ cup boiling water and a dash of lemon juice. Cover and microwave for 4½–5 minutes for a 450g/1lb fish, 8½–10½ minutes for a 900g/2lb fish; 11–14½ minutes for a 1.5kg/3–3½lb fish; and 14½–18½ minutes for a 1.75kg/4–4½lb fish, rotating 3 times during cooking. Leave to stand, covered, for 5 minutes before serving.
SCALLOPS steamed fresh	450g/1lb	MEDIUM	Remove from their shells. Place in a shallow microwaveproof dish and cover with absorbent kitchen paper. Microwave for 8–12 minutes, rearranging once, halfway through cooking. Leave to stand, covered, for 3 minutes before serving.
SHRIMPS AND PRAWNS to boil	450g/1lb 900g/2lb	HIGH	Rinse and place in a microwaveproof dish with 600ml/1 pint/2½ cups water, a dash of vinegar or lemon juice and a bay leaf if liked. Cover and microwave for 6–8 minutes for 450g/1lb; 8–10 minutes for 900g/2lb, stirring once halfway through cooking. Leave to stand, covered, for 3 minutes before draining and shelling.

SOLE
steamed fillets — 450g/1lb — HIGH — Arrange fish fillets in a microwaveproof dish so that the thinner tail ends are to the centre of the dish. Dot with a little butter, season and add a dash of lemon juice. Cover and microwave for 4–6 minutes, rearranging once half-way through cooking. Leave to stand, covered, for 3 minutes before serving.

SMOKED HADDOCK
steamed fillets — 450g/1lb — HIGH — Arrange fish fillets in a microwaveproof dish so that the thinner tail ends are to the centre of the dish. Dot with butter, sprinkle with seasoning and add a dash of lemon juice. Cover and microwave for 5–6 minutes, rearranging once halfway through cooking. Leave the fish to stand, covered, for 3 minutes before serving.

poached fillets — 450g/1lb — HIGH — Place the fillets in a shallow microwaveproof dish with the thinner tail ends to the centre. Pour over 120ml/4fl oz/½ cup milk, dot with a little butter and season to taste. Cover and microwave for 5–6 minutes, rearranging once halfway through cooking. Leave to stand, covered, for 3 minutes before serving.

TROUT
whole — 2 x 250g/9oz
4 x 250g/9oz — HIGH — Clean and gut before cooking. Place in a shallow microwaveproof dish. Slash the skin in several places to prevent bursting during cooking. Dot with butter if liked and season to taste. Cover and microwave for 4–5 minutes for 2 x 250g/9oz trout; and 8–9 minutes for 4 x 250g/9oz trout, turning over once halfway through cooking. Leave the fish to stand, covered, for 5 minutes before serving.

WHITING
steamed fillets — 450g/1lb — HIGH — Arrange fish fillets in a microwaveproof dish so that the thinner tail ends are to the centre of the dish. Dot with a little butter, sprinkle with seasoning and add a dash or two of lemon juice. Cover and microwave for 4–6 minutes, rearranging once halfway through cooking. Leave to stand, covered, for 3 minutes before serving.

Monkfish with Mexican Salsa.

Cooking Poultry and Game

CHICKEN whole roast fresh chicken	1kg/2¼lb 1.5kg/3–3½lb 1.75kg/4–4½lb	HIGH	Rinse, dry and truss the chicken into a neat shape. Season and calculate the cooking time after weighing (and stuffing). Cook breast-side down for half of the cooking time and breast-side up for the remaining cooking time. Brush with a browning agent if liked and shield the wing tips with foil if necessary. Microwave for 12–16 minutes for a 1kg/2¼lb chicken; 18–24 minutes for a 1.5kg/3–3½lb chicken; 25–36 minutes for a 1.75kg/4–4½lb chicken. Cover with foil and leave to stand for 10–15 minutes before carving.
portions	1 x 225g/8oz portion 2 x 225g/8oz portions 4 x 225g/8oz portions	HIGH	Prick with a fork and brush with a browning agent if liked. Alternatively, crisp and brown under a preheated hot grill after cooking. Cover with buttered greaseproof paper to cook. Microwave for 5–7 minutes for 225g/8oz portion; 10–12 minutes for 2 x 225g/8oz portions; 18–24 minutes for 4 x 225g/8oz portions. Leave to stand, covered, for 5–10 minutes before serving.
drumsticks	2 4 8	HIGH	Prick with a fork and brush with a browning agent if liked. Alternatively, crisp and brown under a preheated hot grill after cooking. Cover with buttered greaseproof paper to cook. Microwave for 3–5 minutes for 2 drumsticks; 8–9 minutes for 4 drumsticks; 16–19 minutes for 8 drumsticks. Leave to stand, covered, for 5–10 minutes before serving.
thighs	8	HIGH	Prick with a fork and brush with a browning agent if liked. Alternatively, crisp and brown under a preheated hot grill after cooking. Cover with buttered greaseproof paper to cook. Microwave 8 thighs for 17–20 minutes. Leave to stand, covered, for 5–10 minutes before serving.
breasts	2 4	HIGH	Prick with a fork and brush with a browning agent if liked. Alternatively, crisp and brown under a preheated hot grill after cooking. Cover with buttered greaseproof paper to cook. Microwave for 2–3 minutes for 2 breasts; 3½–4 minutes for 4 breasts. Leave to stand, covered, for 5–10 minutes before serving.
livers, fresh or thawed frozen	225g/8oz 450g/1lb	HIGH	Rinse well and prick to prevent bursting during cooking. Place in a microwaveproof dish with a knob of butter. Cover loosely and microwave for 2–3 minutes for 225g/8oz; and 5–6 minutes for 450g/1lb, stirring twice during cooking. Leave to stand for 2 minutes before serving or using.
DUCK whole roast fresh duck	1.75kg/4–4½lb 2.25kg/5–5¼lb per 450g/1lb	HIGH	Rinse, dry and truss the duck into a neat shape, securing any tail-end flaps of skin to the main body. Prick thoroughly and place on a rack or upturned saucer in a microwaveproof dish for cooking. Cook breast-side down for half of the cooking time, and breast-side up for the remaining cooking time. Microwave for 28–32 minutes for a 1.75kg/4–4½lb duck; 35–40 minutes for a 2.25kg/5–5¼lb duck; or calculate times at 7–8 minutes per 450g/1lb. Drain away excess fat 3 times during cooking and shield tips, tail end and legs with foil if necessary. Cover with foil and leave to stand for 10–15 minutes before serving. Crisp the skin under a preheated hot grill if liked.
GAME BIRDS whole roast	1 x 450g/1lb 2 x 450g/1lb 1 x 900g/2lb 2 x 900g/2lb	HIGH	Rinse, dry and truss the birds into a neat shape. Brush with a browning agent if liked. Cover with greaseproof paper to cook. Microwave for 9–10 minutes for 450g/1lb bird; 18–22 minutes for 2 x 450g/1lb birds; 20–22 minutes for 900g/2lb bird; and 35–40 minutes for 2 x 900g/2lb birds, turning over twice during cooking. Leave to stand, covered, for 5 minutes before serving.

TURKEY			
whole roast fresh	2.75kg/6lb 4kg/9lb 5.5kg/12lb larger birds over 5.5kg/12lb *per* *450g/1lb*	HIGH	Rinse, dry and stuff the turkey if liked. Truss into a neat shape and weigh to calculate the cooking time. Brush with melted butter or browning agent if liked. Divide the cooking time into quarters and cook breast-side down for the first quarter, on one side for the second quarter, on the remaining side for the third quarter and breast-side up for the final quarter. Shield any parts that start to cook faster than others with small strips of foil. Microwave for 42 minutes for a 2.75kg/6lb bird; 63 minutes for a 4kg/9lb bird; 84 minutes for a 5.5kg/12lb bird; or allow 7 minutes per 450g/1lb for larger birds. When cooked, cover with foil and leave to stand for 10–25 minutes (depending upon size of bird) before carving.
drumsticks	2 x 350g/12oz	HIGH *then* MEDIUM	Place on a roasting rack, meaty sections downwards. Baste with a browning agent if liked. Cover and microwave on HIGH for 5 minutes, then on MEDIUM for 13–15 minutes, turning once. Leave to stand, covered, for 5 minutes before serving.
breasts	2 x 225g/8oz breasts 4 x 225g/8oz breasts	MEDIUM	Beat out flat if preferred and place in a shallow dish. Baste with browning agent if liked. Microwave for 8–10 minutes for 2 x 225g/8oz breasts; and 16–18 minutes for 4 x 225g/8oz breasts, turning over once. Leave to stand for 2–3 minutes before serving.

Chicken Roll.

Turkey Lasagne.

Cooking Meat

BACON back and streaky rashers	4 rashers 450g/1lb	HIGH	Place small quantities between sheets of kitchen paper, larger quantities on a plate or microwaveproof bacon rack covered with kitchen paper. Microwave for 3½–4 minutes for 4 rashers; and 12–14 minutes for 450g/1lb, turning over once. Leave to stand for 1–2 minutes before serving.
joint	900g/2lb joint	HIGH	Remove any skin and score the fat into a diamond pattern. Sprinkle with a little brown sugar and stud with cloves if liked. Place on a microwaveproof roasting rack or upturned saucer in a dish. Microwave for 20–24 minutes, rotating the dish twice. Leave to stand, covered with foil, for 10–15 minutes before serving.
BEEF roast joint	per 450g/1lb	HIGH *then* MEDIUM	Ideally place the joint on a microwaveproof roasting rack or upturned saucer inside a roasting bag. Calculate the cooking time according to weight and microwave on HIGH for the first 5 minutes then on MEDIUM for the remaining time. Turn the joint over halfway through the cooking time.

per 450g/1lb

topside or sirloin (boned and rolled)	
rare	8–9 minutes
medium	11–12 minutes
well done	15–16 minutes
forerib or back rib (on the bone)	
rare	7–8 minutes
medium	13–14 minutes
well done	15 minutes
forerib or back rib (boned and rolled)	
rare	11–12 minutes
medium	13–14 minutes
well done	15–16 minutes

Cover with foil after cooking and leave to stand for 10–15 minutes before carving.

minced beef	450g/1lb	HIGH	Place in a microwaveproof dish, cover and microwave for 10–12 minutes, breaking up and stirring twice.
hamburgers	1 x 115g/4oz 2 x 115g/4oz 3 x 115g/4oz 4 x 115g/4oz	HIGH	Ideally cook in a preheated browning dish. If this isn't possible then cook on a roasting rack and increase the times slightly. Microwave for 2½–3 minutes for 1; 3½–4 minutes for 2; 4½–5 minutes for 3; and 5–5½ minutes for 4, turning over once halfway through the cooking time. Leave to stand for 2–3 minutes before serving.
meatloaf	450g/1lb loaf	HIGH	Place your favourite 450g/1lb seasoned beef mixture in a microwaveproof loaf dish, packing in firmly and levelling the surface. Microwave for 7 minutes, allow to stand for 5 minutes, then microwave for a further 5 minutes. Leave to stand, covered with foil, for 3 minutes before serving.
steaks	2 x 225g/8oz rump, sirloin or fillet steaks 4 x 225g/8oz rump, sirloin or fillet steaks	HIGH	Cook with or without the use of a browning dish. If cooking without, then brush with a browning agent if liked prior to cooking. Place in a lightly oiled microwaveproof dish and turn over halfway through the cooking time. Microwave for 5–5½ minutes for 2 x 225g/8oz steaks; and 7½–8½ minutes for 4 x 225g/8oz steaks.

If using a browning dish then preheat first, add a little oil and brush to coat the base. Add the steaks, pressing down well. Turn the steaks over halfway through the cooking time. Microwave for 2¼–2½ minutes for 2 x 225g/8oz steaks; and 3½–4 minutes for 4 x 225g/8oz steaks. Leave to stand for 1–2 minutes before serving.

GAMMON

braised steaks	4 x 115g/4oz steaks	HIGH	Remove the rind and scissor-snip the fat off the gammon steaks. Place in a large shallow microwaveproof dish. Add 150ml/¼ pint/⅔ cup wine, cider or fruit juice (and marinate for 1 hour if liked). Microwave for 4 minutes, rearranging once. Leave to stand, covered, for 5 minutes before serving.
raw joint	per 450g/1lb	HIGH	Place in a pierced roasting bag in a microwaveproof dish. Microwave for 12–14 minutes per 450g/1lb, turning over halfway through the cooking time. Cover with foil and leave to stand for 10 minutes before carving.

KIDNEYS

fresh lamb's, pig's or ox	115g/4oz 225g/8oz 450g/1lb	HIGH	Halve and core the kidneys. Preheat a browning dish. Add 5ml/1 tsp oil and the kidneys. Microwave for 4 minutes for 115g/4oz; 6–8 minutes for 225g/8oz; and 12–15 minutes for 450g/1lb, turning and rearranging twice. Leave to stand, covered, for 3 minutes before serving.

LAMB

roast joint	per 450g/1lb	HIGH *then* MEDIUM	Place the joint on a microwaveproof roasting rack or upturned saucer inside a dish and shield any thin or vulnerable areas with a little foil. Calculate the cooking time according to weight and microwave on HIGH for the first 5 minutes, then on MEDIUM for the remaining time. Turn the joint over halfway through the cooking time.

per 450g/1lb

leg joint with bone

rare	8–10 minutes
medium	10–12 minutes
well done	12–14 minutes

boned leg joints

rare	10–12 minutes
medium	13–15 minutes
well done	16–18 minutes

shoulder joints

rare	7–9 minutes
medium	9–11 minutes
well done	11–13 minutes

chops and steaks	2 loin chops 4 loin chops 2 chump chops 4 chump chops	HIGH	Brush with a browning agent if liked, or cook in a browning dish. Microwave for 6–7 minutes for 2 loin chops; 8–9 minutes for 4 loin chops; 6–8 minutes for 2 chump chops; and 8–10 minutes for 4 chump chops, turning over halfway through the cooking time. Leave to stand for 2–3 minutes before serving.
rack	1.2kg/2–2½lb rack with 7 ribs	HIGH	Chop rack in half and place both pieces together, bones interleaved guard-of-honour style, then tie in place. Place on a microwaveproof roasting rack. Microwave for 12 minutes for rare; 13 minutes for medium; and 14½–15 minutes for well-done lamb, rotating the dish every 3 minutes. Cover with foil and leave to stand for 10 minutes before carving.

LIVER

fresh lamb's liver	450g/1lb	HIGH	Preheat a browning dish. Add 15ml/1 tbsp oil and 15g/½oz/1 tbsp butter. Add sliced, washed and dried liver, pressing down well. Microwave for 1 minute, turn over and microwave for a further 4–5 minutes, rearranging once. Leave to stand for 2 minutes before serving.

PORK

roast joint	per 450g/1lb	HIGH *or* MEDIUM	Place the joint in a microwaveproof dish on a rack if possible. Times are given for roasting on HIGH or MEDIUM. Both methods work well but the latter tends to give a crisper crackling. Turn the joint over halfway through cooking. Brown and crisp under a preheated hot grill after cooking if liked and before the standing time. Calculate the cooking time according to weight and microwave for: *per 450g/1lb* loin, leg and hand joints on bone HIGH 8–9 minutes *or* MEDIUM 12–14 minutes loin and leg joints (boned) HIGH 8–10 minutes *or* MEDIUM 13–15 minutes Cover with foil after cooking and leave to stand for 10–20 minutes before carving.
chops	2 loin chops 4 loin chops 2 chump chops 4 chump chops	HIGH	Brush with a browning agent if liked, or cook in a browning dish. Microwave for 4–5 minutes for 2 loin chops; 6–8 minutes for 4 loin chops; 8–10 minutes for 2 chump chops; and 11–13 minutes for 4 chump chops, turning over once halfway through cooking. Leave to stand for 5 minutes before serving.
pork fillet or tenderloin	350g/12oz	HIGH *then* MEDIUM	Shield the narrow, thin ends of the fillet with a little foil. Place on a microwaveproof roasting rack or upturned saucer in a dish. Microwave on HIGH for 3 minutes, then on MEDIUM for 10–15 minutes, turning over once. Leave to stand, covered with foil, for 5–10 minutes before serving.
sausages standard 50g/2oz size	2 4 8	HIGH	Prick and place on a microwaveproof roasting rack in a dish if possible. Brush with a browning agent if liked or cook in a preheated browning dish. Microwave for 2½ minutes for 2; 4 minutes for 4; and 5 minutes for 8 sausages, turning over once halfway through the cooking time. Leave to stand for 2 minutes before serving.

VEAL

roast joint	per 450g/1lb	HIGH *or* MEDIUM	Place the joint on a microwaveproof rack or upturned saucer in a dish. Times are given for cooking on HIGH *or* MEDIUM. Both methods work well, but the latter is ideal for less-tender cuts or large joints. Calculate the cooking time according to weight and microwave for: *per 450g/1lb* HIGH 8½–9 minutes *or* MEDIUM 11–12 minutes Turn the joint over halfway through the cooking time. Cover with foil after cooking and leave to stand for 15–20 minutes before carving.

Beef and Lentil Pie.

Cooking Vegetables

ARTICHOKES			
globe	1 2 4	HIGH	Discard the tough, outer leaves. Snip the tops off the remaining leaves and trim the stems to the base. Wash and stand upright in a microwaveproof bowl. Pour over the water and lemon juice for 90ml/6 tbsp water and 7.5ml/1½ tsp lemon juice for 1; 120ml/4fl oz/½ cup water and 15ml/1 tbsp lemon juice for 2; and 150ml/¼ pint/⅔ cup water and 30ml/2 tbsp lemon juice for 4. Cover and microwave for 5–6 minutes for 1; 10–11 minutes for 2; and 15–18 minutes for 4, basting and rearranging twice. Leave to stand for 5 minutes before serving.
Jerusalem	450g/1lb	HIGH	Peel and cut into even-size pieces. Place in a microwaveproof bowl with 60ml/4 tbsp water or 25g/1oz/2 tbsp butter. Cover and microwave for 8–10 minutes, stirring once. Leave to stand, covered, for 3–5 minutes before serving.
ASPARAGUS			
fresh whole spears	450g/1lb	HIGH	Prepare and arrange in a shallow microwaveproof dish with pointed tops to the centre. Add 120ml/4fl oz/½ cup water. Cover and microwave for 12–14 minutes, rearranging the spears half way through the time but still keeping the tips to the centre of the dish.
fresh cut spears	450g/1lb	HIGH	Prepare and place in a large shallow microwaveproof dish. Add 120ml/4fl oz/½ cup water. Cover and microwave for 9–11 minutes, rearranging once. Leave to stand, covered, for 5 minutes before serving.
AUBERGINES			
fresh cubes	450g/1lb	HIGH	Cut unpeeled aubergine into 2cm/¾in cubes. Place in a microwaveproof bowl with 25g/1oz/2 tbsp butter. Cover and microwave for 7–10 minutes, stirring every 3 minutes. Leave to stand, covered, for 4 minutes. Season *after* cooking.
fresh whole	225g/8oz 2 x 225g/8oz	HIGH	Peel off stalks, rinse and dry. Brush with a little oil and prick. Place on kitchen paper and microwave for 3–4 minutes for 1 aubergine; 4–6 minutes for 2, turning over once. Leave to stand for 4 minutes. Scoop out flesh and use as required.
BEANS			
fresh green	225g/8oz whole 450g/1lb whole 225g/8oz cut 450g/1lb cut	HIGH	Place whole or cut beans in a microwaveproof bowl and add 30ml/2 tbsp water. Cover and microwave for 8–10 minutes for 225g/8oz whole beans; 15–18 minutes for 450g/1lb whole beans; 7–9 minutes for 225g/8oz cut beans; and 12–15 minutes for 450g/1lb cut beans, stirring once. Leave to stand, covered, for 2–3 minutes before serving.
fresh baby green whole or French whole	225g/8oz 450g/1lb	HIGH	Place in a microwaveproof bowl with 30ml/2 tbsp water. Cover and microwave for 7–9 minutes for 225g/8oz; 12–15 minutes for 450g/1lb, stirring 3 times. Leave to stand, covered, for 2–3 minutes, before serving.
fresh sliced runner beans	225g/8oz 450g/1lb	HIGH	Place in a microwaveproof bowl with 30ml/2 tbsp water. Cover and microwave for 7–9 minutes for 225g/8oz; 12–15 minutes for 450g/1lb, stirring 3–4 times. Leave to stand, covered, for 2–3 minutes before serving.
fresh shelled broad beans	225g/8oz 450g/1lb	HIGH	Place in a microwaveproof bowl and add the water: 75ml/5 tbsp for 225g/8oz beans; and 120ml/4fl oz/½ cup for 450g/1lb beans. Cover and microwave for 5–7 minutes for 225g/8oz; 6–10 minutes for 450g/1lb, stirring once. Leave to stand, covered, for 2–3 minutes before serving.
BEETROOT			
fresh	4 medium	HIGH	Wash the beetroot and pierce the skin with a fork but do not peel. Place in a shallow microwaveproof dish with 60ml/4 tbsp water. Cover loosely and microwave for 14–16 minutes, rearranging twice. Leave to stand, covered, for 5 minutes before removing skins to serve or use.

BROCCOLI fresh spears	225g/8oz 450g/1lb	HIGH	Place spears in a large shallow microwaveproof dish with tender heads to centre of dish. Add 60ml/4 tbsp water. Cover and microwave for 4–5 minutes for 225g/8oz; 8–9 minutes for 450g/1lb, rotating the dish once. Leave to stand, covered, for 2–4 minutes before serving.
fresh pieces	225g/8oz 450g/1lb	HIGH	Cut into 2.5cm/1in pieces. Place in a microwaveproof bowl with 60ml/4 tbsp water. Cover and microwave for 4½–5 minutes for 225g/8oz; 8½–9½ minutes for 450g/1lb, stirring once. Leave to stand, covered, for 3–5 minutes before serving.
BRUSSELS SPROUTS fresh	450g/1lb 900g/2lb	HIGH	Remove outer leaves, trim and cross-cut base. Place in a microwaveproof dish and add water: 60ml/4 tbsp for 450g/1lb; 120ml/4/fl oz/½ cup for 900g/2lb. Cover and microwave for 6–7 minutes for 450g/1lb; 12–14 minute for 900g/2lb, stirring once. Leave to stand, covered, for 3–5 minutes before serving.
CABBAGE fresh	225g/8oz 450g/1lb	HIGH	Core and shred, and place in a large microwaveproof dish. Add water: 60ml/4 tbsp for 225g/8oz; 120ml/4/fl oz/½ cup for 450g/1lb. Cover and microwave for 7–9 minutes for 225g/8oz; 9–11 minutes for 450g/1lb, stirring once. Leave to stand, covered, for 2 minutes before serving.
CARROTS fresh baby whole and sliced	450g/1lb whole 450g/1lb sliced	HIGH	Place in a microwaveproof dish with 60ml/4 tbsp water. Cover and microwave for 12–14 minutes for whole; 10–12 minutes for sliced. Leave to stand, covered, for 3–5 minutes before serving.
CAULIFLOWER fresh whole	675g/1½lb	MEDIUM	Trim but leave whole, and place floret-side down in a microwaveproof dish with 250ml/8fl oz/1 cup water. Cover and microwave for 16–17 minutes, turning over once. Leave to stand for 3–5 minutes before serving.
fresh florets	225g/8oz 450g/1lb	HIGH	Place in a microwaveproof dish with water: 45ml/3 tbsp for 225g/8oz; 60ml/4 tbsp for 450g/1lb. Cover and microwave for 7–8 minutes for 225g/8oz; 10–12 minutes for 450g/1lb, stirring once. Leave to stand for 3 minutes before serving.
CELERY fresh sliced	1 head (about 9 stalks)	HIGH	Slice into 5mm/¼in pieces and place in a shallow microwaveproof dish with 30ml/2 tbsp water and 25g/1oz/2 tbsp butter. Cover and microwave for 5–6 minutes, stirring once. Leave to stand, covered, for 3 minutes before serving.
fresh celery hearts	4 hearts	HIGH	Halve each celery heart lengthways and place in a shallow microwaveproof dish. Add 30ml/2 tbsp water and a knob of butter if liked. Cover and microwave for 4½–5 minutes, turning once. Leave to stand, covered, for 3 minutes before serving.
CHINESE CABBAGE fresh	450g/1lb	HIGH	Slice and place in a large microwaveproof dish. Add 30–45ml/2–3 tbsp water. Cover and microwave for 6–8 minutes, stirring once. Leave to stand, covered, for 3–5 minutes. Season after cooking.
COURGETTES fresh	225g/8oz 450g/1lb	HIGH	Top and tail, and slice thinly. Place in a microwaveproof dish with butter: 25g/1oz/2 tbsp for 225g/8oz; 40g/1½oz/3 tbsp for 450g/1lb. Cover loosely and microwave for 4–6½ minutes for 225g/8oz; 6–8 minutes for 450g/1lb, stirring once. Leave to stand, covered, for 2–3 minutes before serving.

CURLY KALE fresh	450g/1lb	HIGH	Remove the thick stalk and stems, then shred. Place in a microwaveproof bowl with 150ml/¼ pint/⅔ cup water. Cover and microwave for 15–17 minutes, stirring every 5 minutes. Leave to stand for 2 minutes before serving.
FENNEL fresh sliced	450g/1lb	HIGH	Place in a microwaveproof bowl with 45ml/3 tbsp water. Cover and microwave for 9–10 minutes, stirring once. Leave to stand, covered, for 2–3 minutes before serving.
KOHLRABI fresh sliced	450g/1lb 900g/2lb	HIGH	Trim away the root ends and stems, scrub and peel the bulb and cut into 5mm/¼in slices. Place in a microwaveproof bowl with water: 45ml/3 tbsp for 450g/1lb; and 75ml/5 tbsp for 900g/2lb. Cover and microwave for 5–6 minutes for 450g/1lb; 9–11 minutes for 900g/2lb, stirring twice. Leave to stand, covered, for 3–4 minutes. Drain to serve.
LEEKS fresh whole	450g/1lb 900g/2lb	HIGH	Trim and slice from the top of the white to the green leaves in 2–3 places. Wash thoroughly and place in a microwaveproof dish with water: 45ml/3 tbsp for 450g/1lb; and 75ml/5 tbsp for 900g/2lb. Cover and microwave for 3–5 minutes for 450g/1lb; 6–8 minutes for 900g/2lb, rearranging twice. Leave to stand, covered, for 3–5 minutes before serving.
fresh sliced	450g/1lb	HIGH	Place in a microwaveproof dish with 45ml/3 tbsp water. Cover and microwave for 8–10 minutes, stirring once. Leave to stand, covered, for 2–3 minutes before serving.
MANGETOUTS fresh	115g/4oz 225g/8oz	HIGH	Trim and place in a microwaveproof bowl with water: 15ml/1 tbsp for 115g/4oz; 30ml/2 tbsp for 225g/8oz. Cover and microwave for 3–4 minutes for 115g/4oz; and 4–5 minutes for 225g/8oz, stirring once. Leave to stand, covered, for 2 minutes before serving.
MARROW fresh	450g/1lb	HIGH	Peel, remove seeds and cut into small neat dice. Place in a microwaveproof dish without water. Cover loosely and microwave for 7–10 minutes, stirring once. Leave to stand, covered, for 2–3 minutes before serving.
MUSHROOMS fresh whole	225g/8oz 450g/1lb	HIGH	Trim and wipe mushrooms. Place in a microwaveproof dish with water or butter: 25g/1oz/2 tbsp butter or 30ml/2 tbsp water for 225g/8oz mushrooms; and 40g/1½oz/3 tbsp butter or 45ml/3 tbsp water for 450g/1lb mushrooms. Cover and microwave for 3–4 minutes for 225g/8oz; and 4–5 minutes for 450g/1lb, stirring twice. Leave to stand for 1–2 minutes before serving. Season after cooking.
fresh sliced	225g/8oz 450g/1lb	HIGH	As above but microwave for 2–3 minutes for 225g/8oz mushrooms; and 3–4 minutes for 450g/1lb mushrooms.
OKRA fresh	450g/1lb	HIGH	Top and tail, and sprinkle lightly with salt. Leave to drain for 30 minutes. Rinse and place in a microwaveproof dish with 30ml/2 tbsp water or 25g/1oz/2 tbsp butter. Cover and microwave for 8–10 minutes, stirring once. Leave to stand, covered, for 3 minutes before serving.
ONIONS fresh whole	450g/1lb or 4 medium	HIGH	Peel and place in a microwaveproof dish. Cover and microwave for 10–12 minutes, rearranging and rotating once. Leave to stand, covered, for 2 minutes before serving.
fresh sliced	450g/1lb	HIGH	Peel and cut into thin wedges or slices. Place in a microwaveproof dish with 25g/1oz/2 tbsp butter and 30ml/2 tbsp water. Cover loosely and microwave for 7–10 minutes, stirring once. Leave to stand, covered, for 5 minutes before serving.

PAK CHOI (or bok choy cabbage)	450g/1lb	HIGH	Slice stalks and leaves and place in a large microwaveproof dish. Add 30ml/ 2 tbsp water and microwave for 6–8 minutes, stirring once. Leave to stand for 3–5 minutes before serving.
PARSNIPS fresh whole	450g/1lb	HIGH	Peel and prick with a fork. Arrange in a microwaveproof dish with tapered ends to the centre. Dot with 15g/½oz/1 tbsp butter and add 45ml/3 tbsp water and 15ml/1 tbsp lemon juice. Cover and microwave for 9–12 minutes, rearranging once. Leave to stand, covered, for 3 minutes before serving.
fresh slices	450g/1lb	HIGH	Peel and slice. Place in a microwaveproof dish with 15g/½oz/1 tbsp butter, 45ml/3 tbsp water and 15ml/1 tbsp lemon juice. Cover and microwave for 9–12 minutes, stirring twice. Leave to stand, covered, for 3 minutes before serving.
PEAS fresh	115g/4oz 225g/8oz 450g/1lb	HIGH	Place shelled peas in a microwaveproof bowl with butter and water: 15g/½oz/ 1 tbsp butter and 10ml/2 tsp water for 115g/4oz peas; 25g/1oz/2 tbsp butter and 15ml/1 tbsp water for 225g/8oz peas; and 50g/2oz/4 tbsp butter and 30ml/2 tbsp water for 450g/1lb peas. Cover and microwave for 3 minutes for 115g/4oz; 4–5 minutes for 225g/8oz; and 6–8 minutes for 450g/1lb, stirring once. Leave to stand, covered, for 3–5 minutes before serving.
POTATOES mashed or creamed	900g/2lb	HIGH	Peel and cut into 1.5cm/⅝in cubes. Place in a microwaveproof bowl with 75ml/ 5 tbsp water. Cover and microwave for 11–13 minutes, stirring once. Leave to stand, covered, for 5 minutes. Drain and mash with butter and seasoning to taste.
new potatoes or old, peeled and quartered	450g/1lb	HIGH	Scrub and scrape new potatoes if liked. Peel and quarter old potatoes. Place in a microwaveproof dish with 60ml/4 tbsp water. Cover and microwave for 7–10 minutes for new; and 6–8 minutes for old, stirring once. Leave to stand, covered, for 5 minutes before serving.
jacket baked	175g/6oz 2 x 175g/6oz 3 x 175g/6oz 4 x 175g/6oz	HIGH	Scrub and prick the skin. Place on a double sheet of absorbent kitchen paper. Microwave for 4–6 minutes for 1; 6–8 minutes for 2; 8–12 minutes for 3; 12–15 minutes for 4, turning over once. If cooking more than 2 potatoes, arrange in a ring pattern. Leave to stand for 5 minutes, before serving.
PUMPKIN fresh	450g/1lb	HIGH	Remove the skin, seeds and membrane and cut into 2.5cm/1in cubes. Place in a microwaveproof dish with 15g/½oz/1 tbsp butter. Cover and microwave for 4–6 minutes, stirring twice. Leave to stand for 3 minutes, then season to serve plain, or mash with cream and herbs.
SPINACH fresh	450g/1lb	HIGH	Chop or shred and rinse. Place in a microwaveproof bowl without any extra water. Cover and microwave for 6–8 minutes, stirring once. Leave to stand for 2 minutes before serving. Season after cooking.
SQUASH fresh	450g/1lb	HIGH	Pierce whole squash with a knife several times. Microwave for 3–5 minutes per 450g/1lb until the flesh pierces easily with a skewer. Leave to stand for 5 minutes. Halve, scoop out the seeds and fibres and discard. Serve fresh in chunks or mash with butter.
SWEDES fresh	450g/1lb	HIGH	Peel and cut into 1cm/½in cubes. Place in a microwaveproof bowl with 15g/½oz/1 tbsp butter and 30ml/2 tbsp water. Cover and microwave for 10–12 minutes, stirring twice. Leave to stand, covered, for 4 minutes. Drain to serve.

SWEETCORN

corn on the cob, fresh husked	1 x 175g/6oz 2 x 175g/6oz 3 x 175g/6oz 4 x 175g/6oz	HIGH	Wrap individually in clear film or place in a microwaveproof dish with 60ml/4 tbsp water and cover. Place or arrange evenly in the oven and microwave for 3–4 minutes for 1; 5–6 minutes for 2; 7–8 minutes for 3; and 9–10 minutes for 4, rotating and rearranging once. Leave to stand, covered, for 3–5 minutes before serving.

SWEET POTATOES

fresh	450g/1lb, whole 450g/1lb, cubed	HIGH	If cooking whole, prick the skins and place on absorbent kitchen paper. Microwave for 7–9 minutes, turning twice. Allow to cool for handling and peel away the skins to serve. To cook cubes, place in a microwaveproof bowl with 45ml/3 tbsp water. Cover and microwave for 6–8 minutes, stirring twice. Drain and toss with butter and seasoning. Leave to stand for 2 minutes before serving.

SWISS CHARD

fresh	450g/1lb	HIGH	Remove and discard the thick stalk and shred the leaves. Place in a microwaveproof dish with 150ml/¼ pint/⅔ cup water. Cover and microwave for 5½–6½ minutes, stirring every 3 minutes. Leave to stand for 2 minutes before serving. Season after cooking.

TOMATOES

whole and halves	1 medium 4 medium 4 large (beef)	HIGH	Prick whole and/or halved tomatoes, arrange in a circle on a plate, cut-sides up. Dot with butter and season to taste. Microwave for ½ minute for 1 medium; 2–2½ minutes for 4 medium; and 3½–4 minutes for 4 large (beef) tomatoes, according to size and ripeness. Leave to stand for 1–2 minutes before serving.

TURNIPS

whole	450g/1lb	HIGH	Choose only small to medium turnips. Peel and prick with a fork. Arrange in a ring pattern in a shallow microwaveproof dish. Dot with 15g/½oz/1 tbsp butter and add 45ml/3 tbsp water. Cover and microwave for 14–16 minutes, rearranging once. Leave to stand, covered, for 3 minutes before serving.
sliced or cubed	450g/1lb	HIGH	Place slices or cubes in a microwaveproof dish with 15g/½oz/1 tbsp butter and 45ml/3 tbsp water. Cover and microwave for 11–12 minutes for slices; and 12–14 minutes for cubes. Leave to stand, covered, for 3 minutes before serving.

Ratatouille.

Fruity Brown Rice Salad.

Cooking Frozen Vegetables

ASPARAGUS frozen whole spears	450g/1lb	HIGH	Place in a microwaveproof dish with 120ml/4fl oz/½ cup water. Cover and microwave for 9–12 minutes, rearranging once. Leave to stand for 5 minutes before serving.
BEANS frozen green beans	225g/8oz whole 450g/1lb whole 225g/8oz cut 450g/1lb cut	HIGH	Place in a microwaveproof bowl with water, cover and microwave with 30ml/2tbsp water for 9–10 minutes for 225g/8oz whole beans; 60ml/4 tbsp water and 14–15 minutes for 450g/1lb whole beans; 30ml/2 tbsp water and 6–7 minutes for 225g/8oz cut beans; and 60ml/4 tbsp water and 10–12 minutes for 450g/1lb cut beans, stirring once. Leave to stand, covered, for 2–3 minutes before serving.
frozen baby green or French whole beans	225g/8oz 450g/1lb	HIGH	Place in a microwaveproof bowl with water, cover and microwave with 30ml/2 tbsp water for 8–9 minutes for 225g/8oz beans; and 60ml/4 tbsp water and 13–15 minutes for 450g/1lb beans, stirring 3 times. Leave to stand, covered, for 2–3 minutes before serving.
frozen sliced runner beans	225g/8oz 450g/1lb	HIGH	Place in a microwaveproof bowl with water, cover and microwave with 30ml/2 tbsp water for 6–7 minutes for 225g/8oz beans; and 60ml/4 tbsp water and 10–12 minutes for 450g/1lb beans, stirring twice. Leave to stand, covered, for 2–3 minutes before serving.
frozen shelled broad beans	225g/8oz 450g/1lb	HIGH	Place in a microwaveproof bowl with water, cover and microwave with 60ml/4 tbsp water for 6–7 minutes for 225g/8oz beans; and 120ml/4½fl oz/½ cup and 10–11 minutes for 450g/1lb beans, stirring twice. Leave to stand, covered, for 2–3 minutes before serving.
BROCCOLI frozen spears	450g/1lb	HIGH	Place in a microwaveproof dish with 60ml/4 tbsp water. Cover and microwave for 13–14 minutes, stirring once. Leave to stand, covered, for 2–3 minutes before serving.
BRUSSELS SPROUTS frozen	450g/1lb	HIGH	Place in a microwaveproof dish with 30ml/2 tbsp water. Cover and microwave for 10–11 minutes, stirring once. Leave to stand, covered, for 3–5 minutes before serving.
CABBAGE frozen	225g/8oz 450g/1lb	HIGH	Place in a large microwaveproof dish with water, cover and microwave with 60ml/4 tbsp water for 6–8 minutes for 225g/8oz; and 120ml/4½fl oz/½ cup water and 8–10 minutes for 450g/1lb, stirring once. Leave to stand, covered, for 2 minutes before serving.
CARROTS frozen whole and sliced	450g/1lb whole 450g/1lb sliced	HIGH	Place in a microwaveproof dish with water. Cover and microwave with 30ml/2 tbsp water for 10–12 minutes for whole carrots; and 30ml/2 tbsp water and 8–10 minutes for sliced carrots, stirring once. Leave to stand, covered, for 2–3 minutes before serving.
CAULIFLOWER frozen florets	450g/1lb	HIGH	Place in a microwaveproof dish with 60ml/4 tbsp water. Cover and microwave for 8–9 minutes, stirring once. Leave to stand, covered, for 2–3 minutes before serving.
COURGETTES frozen sliced	450g/1lb	HIGH	Place in a shallow microwaveproof dish with 40g/1½oz/3 tbsp butter if liked. Cover loosely and microwave for 7–8 minutes, stirring once. Leave to stand, covered, for 2–3 minutes before serving.

LEEKS
frozen sliced   450g/1lb   HIGH   Place in a microwaveproof dish with 45ml/3 tbsp water. Cover and microwave for 11–12 minutes, stirring once. Leave to stand, covered, for 2–3 minutes before serving.

MANGETOUTS
frozen   225g/8oz   HIGH   Place in a microwaveproof dish with 30ml/2 tbsp water. Cover and microwave for 3–4 minutes, stirring once. Leave to stand, covered, for 2–3 minutes before serving.

MIXED VEGETABLES
frozen   225g/8oz 450g/1lb   HIGH   Place in a microwaveproof dish with water. Cover and microwave with 30ml/ 2 tbsp water for 4–5 minutes for 225g/8oz; and 30ml/2 tbsp water and 7–8 minutes for 450g/1lb, stirring once. Leave to stand, covered, for 2 minutes before serving.

MUSHROOMS
frozen whole button   115g/4oz 225g/8oz   HIGH   Place in a shallow microwaveproof dish with a knob of butter. Cover and microwave for 3–4 minutes for 115g/4oz; and 5–6 minutes for 225g/8oz, stirring twice. Leave to stand, covered, for 1–2 minutes. Season to taste to serve.

PARSNIPS
frozen whole   450g/1lb   HIGH   Arrange in a shallow microwaveproof dish with tapered ends to centre. Cover and microwave for 9–10 minutes, rearranging once. Toss in butter and seasonings to serve. Leave to stand, covered, for 2–3 minutes before serving.

PEAS
frozen   225g/8oz 450g/1lb   HIGH   Place in a microwaveproof dish with water. Cover and microwave with 30ml/ 2 tbsp water for 4–6 minutes for 225g/8oz; and 60ml/4 tbsp water and 6–8 minutes for 450g/1lb, stirring once. Leave to stand, covered, for 3 minutes.

SPINACH
frozen   275g/10oz packet   HIGH   Place in a microwaveproof dish. Cover and microwave for 7–9 minutes, stirring twice to break up during cooking. Season *after* cooking.

SWEDES
frozen cubed swede   450g/1lb   HIGH   Place in a microwaveproof dish, cover and microwave for 8–10 minutes, stirring twice. Leave to stand, covered, for 2–3 minutes. Toss in butter and seasonings or mash with same to a purée.

SWEETCORN
frozen sweetcorn kernels   450g/1lb   HIGH   Place in a microwaveproof dish with 60ml/4 tbsp water. Cover and microwave for 7–8 minutes, stirring once. Leave to stand, covered, for 2–3 minutes before serving.

Herby Baked Tomatoes.

Mushroom and Fennel Hotpot.

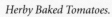

Cooking Pasta, Pulses and Grains

BARLEY pot barley	175g/6oz	HIGH *then* MEDIUM	Toast if liked before cooking. Place in a microwaveproof dish with 1 litre/ 1¾ pints/4 cups boiling water and a pinch of salt if liked. Cover loosely and microwave on HIGH for 3 minutes, then on MEDIUM for 40 minutes. Leave to stand for 5–10 minutes before fluffing with a fork to serve.
BULGUR grains	225g/8oz	HIGH *then* MEDIUM	Place in a microwaveproof dish with 550ml/18fl oz/2¼ cups boiling water and a pinch of salt if liked. Cover loosely and microwave on HIGH for 3 minutes, then on MEDIUM for 9–12 minutes. Leave to stand for 5–10 minutes before fluffing with a fork to serve.
COUSCOUS pre-cooked	350g/12oz	MEDIUM	Place in a microwaveproof dish with 250ml/8fl oz/1 cup boiling water and 50g/2oz/4 tbsp butter. Cover loosely and microwave for 15 minutes. Leave to stand for 5–10 minutes before fluffing with a fork to serve.
DRIED BEANS aduki black black-eyed borlotti broad butter cannellini flageolet haricot mung pinto red kidney soya	225g/8oz	HIGH *then* MEDIUM	Soak dried beans overnight in cold water or hasten soaking by par-cooking in the microwave. Place the dried beans in a microwaveproof bowl with boiling water to cover. Cover and microwave on HIGH for 5 minutes. Leave to stand, covered, for 1½ hours before draining to cook. Place soaked or par-cooked beans in a microwaveproof dish and cover with boiling water. Cover and microwave all beans on HIGH for 10 minutes. Reduce the power to MEDIUM and microwave aduki, black-eyed, mung and pinto beans for 10–15 minutes; and black, borlotti, broad, butter, cannellini, flageolet, haricot, red kidney and soya beans for 20–25 minutes, adding extra boiling water to cover if needed. Drain to use.
DRIED CHICK- PEAS	225g/8oz	HIGH *then* MEDIUM	Soak dried peas overnight or according to packet instructions. Place soaked peas in a microwaveproof dish and cover with boiling water. Cover and microwave on HIGH for 10 minutes, then on MEDIUM for 20–25 minutes, adding extra boiling water to cover if needed. Drain to use.
DRIED WHOLE GREEN PEAS	225g/8oz	HIGH *then* MEDIUM	Soak dried peas overnight or according to packet instructions. Place soaked peas in a microwaveproof dish and cover with boiling water. Cover and microwave on HIGH for 10 minutes, then on MEDIUM for 10–15 minutes, adding extra boiling water to cover if needed. Drain to use.
DRIED SPLIT PEAS	225g/8oz	HIGH	Soak dried peas overnight or according to packet instructions. Place soaked peas in a microwaveproof dish and cover with boiling water. Cover and microwave on HIGH for 10 minutes. Drain to use.
DRIED LENTILS	225g/8oz	HIGH	Place the lentils in a microwaveproof dish with a few seasoning vegetables such as chopped onion, celery, carrot or bouquet garni and a squeeze of lemon juice. Add 900ml/1½ pints/3¾ cups boiling water or stock. Cover and microwave for 15–25 minutes, stirring once halfway through cooking. Cook for the shorter length of time if the lentils are to be served in a salad mixture or as a meal accompaniment, the longer time if the lentils are to be puréed for use.
MILLET	225g/8oz	HIGH *then* MEDIUM	Toast if liked before cooking. Place in a microwaveproof dish with 650ml/ 22fl oz/2¾ cups boiling water and a pinch of salt if liked. Cover loosely and microwave on HIGH for 3 minutes, then on MEDIUM for 12 minutes. Leave to stand for 5–10 minutes before fluffing with a fork to serve.

OATS grains	175g/6oz	HIGH *then* MEDIUM	Toast if liked before cooking. Place in a microwaveproof dish with 750ml/ 1¼ pints/3 cups boiling water and a pinch of salt if liked. Cover loosely and microwave on HIGH for 3 minutes, then on MEDIUM for 20–22 minutes. Leave to stand for 5–10 minutes before fluffing with a fork to serve.
PASTA fresh: egg noodles spaghetti tagliatelle ravioli	225g/8oz	HIGH	Place the pasta in a large microwaveproof dish. Cover with 750ml/ 1¼ pints/3 cups boiling water and add 5ml/1 tsp oil. Cover loosely and microwave for 2–2½ minutes for egg noodles; 4–6 minutes for spaghetti; 2–3 minutes for tagliatelle; and 6–8 minutes for ravioli, stirring once halfway through the cooking time. Leave to stand for 2 minutes before draining to serve.
dried: egg noodles spaghetti tagliatelle short-cut macaroni pasta shapes ravioli	225g/8oz	HIGH	Place the pasta in a large microwaveproof dish. Add a generous 1.2 litres/ 2 pints/5 cups of boiling water and 5ml/1 tsp oil. Cover loosely and microwave: 6 minutes for egg noodles; 10–12 minutes for spaghetti; 6 minutes for tagliatelle; 10 minutes for short-cut macaroni; 10-12 minutes for pasta shapes; and 10 minutes for ravioli, stirring once halfway through the cooking time. Leave to stand for 3–5 minutes before draining to use.
RICE long grain white	115g/4oz 225g/8oz	HIGH *then* MEDIUM	Place the rice in a large microwaveproof dish. Add boiling water: 300ml/ ½ pint/1¼ cups for 115g/4oz rice; and 550ml/18fl oz/2¼ cups for 225g/8oz rice with a pinch of salt and knob of butter if liked. Cover loosely and microwave on HIGH for 3 minutes. Stir well then re-cover and microwave on MEDIUM for 12 minutes. Leave to stand, covered, for 5 minutes before fluffing with a fork to serve.
long grain brown	115g/4oz 225g/8oz	HIGH *then* MEDIUM	Place the rice in a large microwaveproof dish. Add boiling water: 300ml/ ½ pint/1¼ cups for 115g/4oz; 550ml/18fl oz/2¼ cups for 225g/8oz rice with a pinch of salt and knob of butter if liked. Cover loosely and microwave on HIGH for 3 minutes. Stir well then re-cover and microwave on MEDIUM for 25 minutes. Leave to stand, covered, for 5 minutes before fluffing with a fork to serve.
long grain and wild rice mix	400g/14oz packet	HIGH *then* MEDIUM	Place the rice mix in a microwaveproof dish with 650ml/22fl oz/2¾ cups boiling water, a pinch of salt and knob of butter if liked. Cover loosely and microwave on HIGH for 3 minutes. Stir well, re-cover and microwave on MEDIUM for 12 minutes, stirring once. Leave to stand, covered, for 5 minutes before fluffing with a fork to serve.
RYE grains	175g/6oz	HIGH *then* MEDIUM	Soak the rye grains for 6–8 hours in cold water then drain. Place in a microwaveproof dish with 750ml/1¼ pints/3 cups boiling water. Cover loosely and microwave on HIGH for 3 minutes, then on MEDIUM for 40 minutes. Leave to stand 5–10 minutes before fluffing with a fork to serve.
WHEAT grains	175g/6oz	HIGH *then* MEDIUM	Soak wheat grains for 6–8 hours in cold water then drain. Place in a microwaveproof dish with 1 litre/1¾ pints/4 cups boiling water. Cover loosely and microwave on HIGH for 3 minutes, then on MEDIUM for 40 minutes. Leave to stand 5–10 minutes before fluffing with a fork to serve.

Cooking Fruit

APPLES poached in light syrup	450g/1lb	HIGH	Peel, core and slice apples and place in a microwaveproof bowl with 300ml/½ pint/1¼ cups hot sugar syrup. Cover loosely and microwave for 3 minutes, stirring once. Leave to stand, covered, for 5 minutes.
	900g/2lb	HIGH	As above, but microwave for 5–6 minutes.
stewed	450g/1lb	HIGH	Peel, core and slice apples and place in a microwaveproof bowl with 115g/4oz/½ cup sugar. Cover loosely and microwave for 6–8 minutes, stirring once. Leave to stand, covered, for 2–3 minutes.
baked	4 large	HIGH	Wash and remove cores from the apples and score around the middle to prevent bursting. Place in a microwaveproof dish, stuff with a little dried fruit if liked. Pour 120ml/4fl oz/½ cup water around fruit and microwave for 9–10 minutes, rearranging once. Leave to stand, covered, for 3–4 minutes before serving.
APRICOTS poached in light syrup	6–8	HIGH	Skin, halve and stone, slicing if preferred. Place in a microwaveproof bowl with 300ml/½ pint/1¼ cups hot sugar syrup. Cover loosely and microwave for 3–4 minutes, stirring once. Leave to stand, covered, for 5 minutes.
stewed	6–8	HIGH	Stone and wash. Place in a microwaveproof bowl, sprinkle with 115g/4oz/½ cup sugar. Cover and microwave for 6–8 minutes, stirring once. Leave to stand, covered, for 5 minutes before serving.
BANANAS baked	2 large	HIGH	Peel and halve the bananas lengthways. Place in a microwaveproof dish with a little sugar and fruit juice. Microwave for 3–4 minutes, stirring or rearranging twice.
BLACKBERRIES poached in light syrup	450g/1lb	HIGH	Hull and rinse. Place in a microwaveproof bowl with 300ml/½ pint/1¼ cups hot sugar syrup. Cover loosely and microwave for 2 minutes, stirring once. Leave to stand, covered, for 5 minutes.
BLACKCURRANTS fresh	450g/1lb	HIGH	Top and tail and place in a microwaveproof dish with 115g/4oz/½ cup sugar and 30ml/2 tbsp water. Cover loosely and microwave for 5 minutes, stirring once. Leave to stand, covered, for 5 minutes.
CHERRIES poached in light syrup	450g/1lb	HIGH	Prick and stone if preferred. Place in a microwaveproof bowl with 300ml/½ pint/1¼ cups of hot sugar syrup. Cover loosely and microwave for 2–3 minutes, stirring once. Leave to stand, covered, for 5 minutes.
stewed	450g/1lb	HIGH	Stone, wash and place in a microwaveproof bowl with 115g/4oz/½ cup sugar and a little grated lemon rind if liked. Cover and microwave for 4–5 minutes, stirring once. Leave to stand, covered, for 3–5 minutes.
CRANBERRIES cranberry sauce	450g/1lb	HIGH	Place the cranberries, 90ml/6 tbsp water and 350g/12oz/1¾ cups sugar in a large microwaveproof bowl. Cover with vented cling film and microwave for 18–20 minutes, stirring every 6 minutes, until pulpy.
DAMSONS poached in light syrup	450g/1lb, whole or halved	HIGH	Prick whole damsons or halve and stone if preferred. Place in a microwaveproof bowl with 300ml/½ pint/1¼ cups hot sugar syrup. Cover loosely and microwave for 3 minutes for whole damsons; 2 minutes for halves, stirring once. Leave to stand, covered, for 5 minutes.

stewed	450g/1lb	HIGH	Stone and wash. Place in a microwaveproof bowl with 115g/4oz/½ cup sugar and a little grated lemon rind if liked. Cover and microwave for 4–5 minutes, stirring once. Leave to stand, covered, for 3–5 minutes.
GOOSEBERRIES fresh	450g/1lb	HIGH	Top and tail and place in a microwaveproof bowl with 30ml/2 tbsp water. Cover and microwave for 4–6 minutes. Stir in 115g/4oz/½ cup sugar and leave to stand, covered, for 5 minutes.
GREENGAGES poached in light syrup	450g/1lb whole or halved	HIGH	Prick whole greengages or halve and stone if preferred. Place in a microwaveproof bowl with 300ml/½ pint/1¼ cups hot sugar syrup. Cover loosely and microwave for 3 minutes for whole greengages; 2 minutes for halves, stirring once. Leave to stand, covered, for 5 minutes.
stewed	450g/1lb		Stone and wash. Place in a microwaveproof bowl with 115g/4oz/½ cup sugar and a little grated lemon rind if liked. Cover and microwave for 4–5 minutes, stirring once. Leave to stand, covered, for 3–5 minutes.
NECTARINES poached in light syrup	8	HIGH	Skin and prick thoroughly. Place in a microwaveproof bowl with 300ml/½ pint/1¼ cups hot sugar syrup and a dash of lemon juice. Cover loosely and microwave for 6 minutes, stirring once. Leave to stand, covered, for 5 minutes.
stewed	4 medium	HIGH	Stone, wash and slice. Place in a microwaveproof bowl with 115g/4oz/½ cup sugar. Cover and microwave for 4–5 minutes, stirring once. Leave to stand, covered, for 5 minutes.
ORANGES poached in light syrup	4	HIGH	Peel if preferred, or scrub the skin, then finely slice. Place in a microwaveproof bowl with 300ml/½ pint/1¼ cups hot sugar syrup. Cover loosely and microwave for 3 minutes, stirring once. Leave to stand, covered, for 5 minutes.
PEACHES poached in light syrup	4 whole or sliced	HIGH	Skin and prick thoroughly or skin, stone and slice. Place in a microwaveproof bowl with 300ml/½ pint/1¼ cups hot sugar syrup. Cover loosely and microwave for 4 minutes for whole peaches; 3 minutes for slices, stirring once. Leave to stand, covered, for 5 minutes.
stewed	4 medium	HIGH	Stone, wash and slice. Place in a microwaveproof bowl with 115g/4oz/½ cup sugar. Cover and microwave for 4–5 minutes, stirring once. Leave to stand, covered, for 5 minutes.
PEARS poached in light syrup	900g/2lb whole dessert 900g/2lb whole cooking 900g/2lb halved dessert	HIGH	Peel and prick if kept whole, or halve and core. Place in a microwaveproof bowl with 300ml/½ pint/1¼ cups hot sugar syrup. Cover loosely and microwave for 5 minutes for whole dessert pears; 10 minutes for whole cooking pears: and 3 minutes for halved dessert pears, stirring once. Leave to stand, covered, for 5 minutes.
stewed	6 medium	HIGH	Peel, halve and core. Dissolve 75g/3oz/⅓ cup sugar in a little water and pour over the pears. Cover loosely and microwave for 8–10 minutes, stirring once. Leave to stand, covered, for 5 minutes.
PINEAPPLE poached in light syrup	900g/2lb	HIGH	Peel, core and cut into bite-size pieces. Place in a microwaveproof bowl with 300ml/½ pint/1¼ cups hot sugar syrup. Cover loosely and microwave for 5 minutes, stirring once. Leave to stand, covered, for 5 minutes.

PLUMS poached in light syrup	450g/1lb whole or halved	HIGH	Prick if kept whole or halve and stone. Place in a microwaveproof bowl with 300ml/½ pint/1¼ cups hot sugar syrup. Cover loosely and microwave for 3 minutes for whole plums; 2 minutes for halved, stirring once. Leave to stand, covered, for 5 minutes.
stewed	450g/1lb	HIGH	Stone and wash. Place in a microwaveproof bowl with 115g/4oz/½ cup sugar and a little grated lemon rind if liked. Cover and microwave for 4–5 minutes, stirring once. Leave to stand, covered, for 3–5 minutes.
RASPBERRIES poached in light syrup	450g/1lb	HIGH	Hull and rinse. Place in a microwaveproof bowl with 300ml/½ pint/1¼ cups hot sugar syrup. Cover loosely and microwave for 2 minutes, stirring once. Leave to stand, covered, for 5 minutes.
REDCURRANTS fresh	450g/1lb	HIGH	Top and tail and place in a microwaveproof bowl with 115g/4oz/½ cup sugar and 30ml/2 tbsp water. Cover loosely and microwave for 5 minutes, stirring once. Leave to stand for 5 minutes.
RHUBARB fresh	350g/12oz	HIGH	Cut into 2.5cm/1in lengths. Place in a microwaveproof bowl with 30ml/2 tbsp water. Cover loosely and microwave for 6–7 minutes, stirring once. Stir in 115g/4oz/½ cup sugar and 5ml/1 tsp lemon juice. Leave to stand, covered, for 2–3 minutes.
poached in light syrup	450g/1lb	HIGH	Cut into 2.5cm/1in lengths. Place in a microwaveproof bowl with 300ml/½ pint/1¼ cups hot sugar syrup. Cover loosely and microwave for 4 minutes, stirring once. Leave to stand, covered, for 5 minutes.
STRAWBERRIES poached in light syrup	450g/1lb	HIGH	Hull and rinse. Place in a microwaveproof bowl with 300ml/½ pint/1¼ cups hot sugar syrup. Cover loosely and microwave for 2 minutes, stirring once. Leave to stand, covered, for 5 minutes.

SUGAR SYRUP
To make sugar syrup for poaching fruits: place 115g/4oz/½ cup sugar and 300ml/½ pint/1¼ cups water in a microwaveproof jug. Microwave on HIGH for 4–5 minutes, stirring 3 times. Use as required. Makes 300ml/½ pint/1¼ cups.

Hot Bananas with Rum and Raisins.

Poached Pears in Red Wine.

Defrosting Fish and Shellfish

COD frozen steaks	1 x 225g/8oz 2 x 225g/8oz 4 x 225g/8oz	DEFROST	To defrost, place in a microwaveproof dish, cover and microwave for 2–2 ½ minutes for 1 steak; 3–4 minutes for 2 steaks; and 6–7 minutes for 4 steaks, turning over or rearranging once. Leave to stand, covered, for 10 minutes before using.
frozen fillets	450g/1lb	DEFROST	To defrost, place in a microwaveproof dish with the thicker portions to the outer edge. Cover and microwave for 7–8 minutes, rearranging once. Leave to stand for 5 minutes before using.
CRABMEAT frozen	225g/8oz	DEFROST	Leave in wrappings. Microwave for 4 minutes, turning over once. Leave to stand for 2 minutes, then flake to use.
FISHCAKES frozen	4 x 75g/3oz	DEFROST	To defrost, unwrap and place in a shallow microwaveproof dish. Cover and microwave for 5–6½ minutes, rearranging once. Leave to stand for 2 minutes before cooking.
HADDOCK frozen steaks	1 x 225g/8oz 2 x 225g/8oz 4 x 225g/8oz	DEFROST	To defrost, place in a microwaveproof dish, cover and microwave for 2–2½ minutes for 1 steak; 3–4 minutes for 2 steaks; and 6–7 minutes for 4 steaks, turning over or rearranging once. Leave to stand for 10 minutes before using.
frozen fillets	450g/1lb	DEFROST	To defrost, place in a microwaveproof dish with the thicker portions to the outer edge. Cover and microwave for 7–8 minutes, rearranging once. Leave to stand for 5 minutes before using.
HALIBUT frozen steaks	1 x 225g/8oz 2 x 225g/8oz 4 x 225g/8oz	DEFROST	To defrost, place in a microwaveproof dish, cover and microwave for 2–2½ minutes for 1 steak; 3–4 minutes for 2 steaks; and 6–7 minutes for 4 steaks, turning over or rearranging once. Leave to stand for 10 minutes before using.
HERRING frozen whole	per 450g/1lb	DEFROST	To defrost, place in a shallow microwaveproof dish and microwave for 5–7 minutes per 450g/1lb, turning once. Leave to stand for 10 minutes before using.
KIPPERS frozen fillets	175g/6oz boil-in-the-bag	HIGH	To defrost *and* cook, place the frozen boil-in-the-bag on a plate and snip a couple of vents in the bag. Microwave for 5–6 minutes, turning over once. Leave to stand for 2–3 minutes before serving.
LOBSTER frozen whole cooked	per 450g/1lb	DEFROST	To defrost, place in a microwaveproof dish, cover and microwave for 12–15 minutes per 450g/1lb, giving the dish a quarter turn every 2 minutes and turning over after 6 minutes. Leave to stand for 5 minutes before serving.
MACKEREL frozen whole	per 450g/1lb	DEFROST	To defrost, place in a shallow microwaveproof dish and microwave for 5–7 minutes per 450g/1lb, turning over once. Leave to stand for 10 minutes before using.
MUSSELS frozen cooked shelled	225g/8oz	DEFROST	To defrost, spread the mussels out on a plate in a single layer. Microwave for 3½–4 minutes, stirring to rearrange once. Leave to stand for 2 minutes before using.
PLAICE frozen fillets	450g/1lb	DEFROST	To defrost, place in a microwaveproof dish with the thicker portions to the outer edge. Cover and microwave for 7–8 minutes, rearranging once. Leave to stand for 5 minutes before using.

frozen whole	1 x 275g/10oz 2 x 275g/10oz	DEFROST	To defrost, place on a plate, cover and microwave for 4–6 minutes for 1 plaice; and 10–12 minutes for 2 plaice, shielding the tail end with a little foil halfway through cooking if necessary. Leave to stand for 5 minutes before using.
PRAWNS AND SHRIMPS frozen cooked	450g/1lb	DEFROST	To defrost, place in a microwaveproof dish and microwave for 7–8 minutes, stirring twice. Leave to stand for 2–3 minutes before using.
RED OR GREY MULLET frozen whole	2 x 200–250g/7–9oz 4 x 200–250g/7–9oz	DEFROST	To defrost, place in a shallow microwaveproof dish and microwave for 9–11 minutes for 2 whole fish; and 19–21 minutes for 4 whole fish, turning or rearranging twice. Leave to stand for 5 minutes before using.
RED SNAPPER frozen whole	450–550g/1–1½lb	MEDIUM	To defrost individually (for best results), place in a shallow microwaveproof dish, cover and microwave for 2½–3½ minutes, turning over once. Rinse in cold water then pat dry. Leave to stand for 2–3 minutes before using.
SALMON AND SALMON TROUT frozen steaks	2 x 225g/8oz 4 x 225g/8oz 4 x 175g/6oz	DEFROST	To defrost, place in a shallow microwaveproof dish, cover and microwave for 4–5 minutes for 2 x 225g/8oz steaks; 10–12 minutes for 4 x 225g/8oz steaks; and 10 minutes for 4 x 175g/6oz steaks, turning over and rearranging once. Leave to stand, covered, for 5–10 minutes before using.
frozen whole salmon or salmon trout	450g/1lb 900g/2lb 1.5kg/3–3½lb 1.75kg/4–4½lb	DEFROST	To defrost, place in a shallow microwaveproof dish, cover and microwave for 6–8 minutes for a 450g/1lb fish; 12–16 minutes for a 900g/2lb fish; 18–20 minutes for a 1.5kg/3–3½lb fish; and 22–24 minutes for a 1.75kg/4–4½lb fish, turning over and rotating the dish twice. Shield the head and tail with a little foil as necessary. Leave to stand, covered, for 5–10 minutes before using.
SCALLOPS frozen	350g/12oz packet 450g/1lb	DEFROST	To defrost, place in a microwaveproof bowl, cover and microwave for 6–8 minutes for 350g/12oz; and 7½–10 minutes for 450g/1lb, stirring and breaking apart twice. Leave to stand, covered, for 5 minutes before using.
SCAMPI frozen cooked	450g/1lb	DEFROST	To defrost, place in a shallow microwaveproof dish and microwave for 7–8 minutes, stirring twice. Leave to stand, covered, for 5 minutes before using.
SMOKED HADDOCK frozen fillets	175g/6oz boil-in-the-bag	HIGH	To defrost *and* cook, place bag on a plate and snip a couple of vent holes. Microwave for 5–6 minutes, turning over once. Leave to stand for 2–3 minutes before using.
SMOKED SALMON frozen sliced	90–115g/3–4oz packet	DEFROST	To defrost, unwrap the salmon and separate the slices. Arrange evenly on a plate and microwave for 1½–2 minutes, turning once.
SOLE frozen fillets	450g/1lb	DEFROST	To defrost, place in a microwaveproof dish with thicker portions to the outer edge. Cover and microwave for 7–8 minutes, rearranging once. Leave to stand for 5 minutes before using.
TROUT frozen whole	2 x 225–275g/8–10oz 4 x 225–275g/8–10oz	DEFROST	To defrost, place in a shallow microwaveproof dish and microwave for 9–11 minutes for 2 whole fish; and 19–21 minutes for 4 whole fish, turning or rearranging twice. Leave to stand for 5 minutes before using.
WHITING frozen fillets	450g/1lb	DEFROST	To defrost, place in a microwaveproof dish with thicker portions to the outer edge. Cover and microwave for 7–8 minutes, rearranging once. Leave to stand for 5 minutes before using.

Defrosting Poultry and Game

CHICKEN

frozen quarters	2 x 225g/8oz 4 x 225g/8oz	LOW	To defrost, remove any wrappings and place in a microwaveproof dish so that the meatiest parts are to the outer edge. Microwave for 7–9 minutes for 2 x 225g/8oz quarters; and 15 minutes for 4 x 225g/8oz quarters, turning over and rearranging once. Leave to stand for 10 minutes before using.
frozen drumsticks, about 115g/4oz each	2 4 6	LOW	To defrost, remove any wrappings and place in a shallow microwaveproof dish so that the meatiest parts are to the outer edge. Microwave for 4–5 minutes for 2; 7–8 minutes for 4; and 12 minutes for 6 drumsticks, turning over and rearranging once. Leave to stand for 10 minutes before using.
frozen thighs, about 115g/4oz each	4 8	LOW	To defrost, remove any wrappings and place in a shallow microwaveproof dish so that the meatiest parts are to the outer edge. Microwave for 8 minutes for 4 thighs; and 15 minutes for 8 thighs, turning over and rearranging once. Leave to stand for 10 minutes before using.
frozen wings	450g/1lb 900g/2lb	LOW	To defrost, remove any wrappings and place in a shallow microwaveproof dish. Microwave for 8 minutes for 450g/1lb; and 15 minutes for 900g/2lb wings, turning over and rearranging twice. Leave to stand for 10 minutes before using.
frozen boneless breasts	2 x 225g/8oz 4 x 225g/8oz	LOW	To defrost, remove any wrappings and place in a shallow microwaveproof dish. Microwave for 8 minutes for 2 x 225g/8oz breasts; and 15 minutes for 4 x 225g/8oz breasts, turning over and rearranging once. Leave to stand for 10 minutes before using.
frozen whole chicken	1kg/2¼lb 1.5kg/3–3½lb 1.75kg/4–4½lb	DEFROST	To defrost, remove wrappings and place, breast-side down, on a microwaveproof rack or upturned saucer in a shallow dish. Microwave for 12–14 minutes for a 1kg/2¼lb bird; 18–22 minutes for a 1.5kg/3–3½lb bird; and 24–30 minutes for a 1.75kg/4–4½lb bird, turning over halfway through the time and shielding legs, wing tips or hot spots with foil if necessary. Leave to stand for 15 minutes before using. Remove any giblets at the end of the defrosting time.
frozen chicken livers	225g/8oz carton	DEFROST	To defrost, remove from carton and place in a microwaveproof dish. Cover and microwave for 6–8 minutes, separating livers as they soften. Leave to stand, covered, for 5 minutes before using.

DUCK

frozen whole	2.25kg/5–5½lb per 450g/1lb	DEFROST	To defrost, shield the wing tips, tail end and legs with foil as necessary for half of the time. Place breast-side down in a shallow microwaveproof dish and microwave for 10 minutes; turn breast-side up and microwave for a further 15–20 minutes, rotating twice. Stand, covered, for 15 minutes before using. Alternatively, defrost for 5–6 minutes per 450g/1lb.
frozen duck portions	4 x 350–400g/ 12–14oz portions	HIGH *then* DEFROST	To defrost, place in a microwaveproof dish and microwave on HIGH for 7 minutes. Turn over, rearrange and microwave on DEFROST for 10–14 minutes. Leave to stand, covered, for 15 minutes before using.

GAME BIRDS

frozen grouse, guinea fowl, partridge, pheasant, pigeon, quail and woodcock	1 x 450g/1lb 2 x 450g/1lb 1 x 900g/2lb 4 x 450g/1lb	DEFROST	To defrost, place on a plate or in a shallow microwaveproof dish, breast-side down. Cover loosely and microwave for half the recommended times: 6–7 minutes for 450g/1lb bird; 12–14 minutes for 2 x 450g/1lb birds; 12–14 minutes for 900g/2lb bird; and 24–28 minutes for 4 x 450g/1lb birds, turning breast-side up after half the time and rearranging if more than 1 bird. Allow to stand, covered, for 5–10 minutes before using.

GIBLETS

frozen	1 bag from poultry bird	DEFROST	To defrost, place in a microwaveproof bowl, cover and microwave for 2–3 minutes. Use as required.

TURKEY frozen whole	2.75kg/6lb 4kg/9lb 5.5kg/12lb 6.8kg/15lb	MEDIUM	To defrost, place the bird breast-side down in a shallow microwaveproof dish and microwave for a quarter of the time. Turn breast-side up and cook for a further quarter of the time. Shield wing tips and legs with small pieces of foil and turn turkey over, cook for the remaining time. Microwave for 21–33 minutes for a 2.75kg/6lb bird; 32–50 minutes for a 4kg/9lb bird; 42–66 minutes for a 5.5kg/12lb bird; and 53–83 minutes for a 6.8kg/15lb bird, checking for hot spots frequently. Leave to stand, covered, for 30–45 minutes, before using.
frozen drumsticks, about 350–400g/ 12–14oz each	2 4	LOW	To defrost, place in a microwaveproof dish with the meatiest parts to the outer edge. Microwave for 12–16 minutes for 2 drumsticks; and 24–26 minutes for 4 drumsticks, turning over and rearranging once. Leave to stand, covered, for 10 minutes before using.
frozen breasts, about 225g/8oz each	2 4	LOW	To defrost, place in a microwaveproof dish. Microwave for 5–7 minutes for 2 breasts; 10–12 minutes for 4 breasts, turning over and rearranging once. Leave to stand, covered, for 10 minutes before using.

Spiced Chicken with Spinach.

Defrosting Meat

BACON

frozen rashers	225g/8oz vacuum pack	DEFROST	To defrost, place on a plate. Microwave for 2–3 minutes, turning over once.
frozen joint	450g/1lb 900g/2lb	DEFROST	To defrost, if in vacuum pack, then pierce and place on a plate. Microwave for 8 minutes for 450g/1lb joint; 15–17 minutes for 900g/2lb joint, turning over twice. Leave to stand, covered, for 20–30 minutes before using.

BEEF

frozen uncooked joint	per 450g/1lb joints on bone per 450g/1lb boneless joints	DEFROST	To defrost, place joint on a microwaveproof roasting rack or upturned saucer in a dish. Microwave for 5–6 minutes per 450g/1lb for joints on bone; and 10 minutes per 450g/1lb for boneless joints, turning over once. Leave to stand, covered, for 30–45 minutes before using.
frozen mince	225g/8oz 450g/1lb 900g/2lb	DEFROST	To defrost, place in a microwaveproof bowl and microwave for 5 minutes for 225g/8oz; 9–10 minutes for 450g/1lb; and 17–18 minutes for 900g/2lb, breaking up twice during the cooking time. Leave to stand for 5–10 minutes before using.
frozen stewing or braising steak cubes	225g/8oz 450g/1lb	DEFROST	To defrost, place in a shallow microwaveproof dish and microwave for 5–7 minutes for 225g/8oz; 8–10 minutes for 450g/1lb, stirring twice. Leave to stand 5–10 minutes before using.
frozen hamburgers	4 x 115g/4oz	DEFROST	To defrost, place on absorbent kitchen paper and microwave for 10–12 minutes, turning over and rearranging twice. Leave to stand 2–3 minutes before using.
frozen steaks	1 x 175–225g/6–8oz 4 x 115–175g/4–6oz 2 x 225g/8oz	DEFROST	Place on a plate. Cover and microwave for 4 minutes for 1 x 175–225g/6–8oz steak, 4–6 minutes for 4 x 115–175g/4–6oz steaks; and 6–8 minutes for 2 x 225g/8oz steaks; turning over once. Leave to stand, covered, for 5–10 minutes before using.

GAMMON

frozen uncooked joint	450g/1lb 900g/2lb	DEFROST	To defrost, place joint on a plate and microwave for 4–5 minutes for a 450g/1lb joint; and 8–10 minutes for a 900g/2lb joint. Leave to stand, covered, for 10–15 minutes before using.
frozen steaks	2 x 115g/4oz 4 x 115g/4oz	DEFROST	To defrost, place on a plate and microwave for 3–5 minutes for 2 x 115g/4oz steaks; and 7–9 minutes for 4 x 115g/4oz steaks, turning over once. Leave to stand for 5 minutes before using.

HAM

frozen uncooked joint	450g/1lb 900g/2lb	DEFROST	To defrost, place the joint on a plate and microwave for 4–5 minutes for a 450g/1lb joint; and 8–10 minutes for a 900g/2lb joint, turning over once. Leave to stand, covered, for 10–15 minutes before using.
frozen sliced cooked	115g/4oz packet	DEFROST	To defrost, place on a plate and microwave for 3–4 minutes, turning over once. Leave to stand for 5 minutes before using.

KIDNEYS

frozen lamb's, pig's or ox	2 lamb's 4 lamb's 2 pig's 4 pig's 225g/8oz ox 450g/1lb ox	DEFROST	To defrost, place in a microwaveproof bowl, cover and microwave for 1½–2 minutes for 2 lamb's; 4 minutes for 4 lamb's; 4 minutes for 2 pig's; 7–8 minutes for 4 pig's; 6 minutes for 225g/8oz ox; and 9–10 minutes for 450g/1lb ox kidney, rearranging 3 times. Leave to stand, covered, for 5 minutes before using.

LAMB			
frozen chops	2 x 115–175g/4–6oz loin chops 4 x 115–175g/4–6oz loin chops 2 x 115–175g/4–6oz chump chops 4 x 115–175g/4–6oz chump chops	DEFROST	To defrost, place on a microwaveproof roasting rack and microwave for 3–4 minutes for 2 x 115–175g/4–6oz loin chops; 6–8 minutes for 4 x 115–175g/4–6oz loin chops; 3–4 minutes for 2 x 115–175g/4–6oz chump chops; and 6–8 minutes for 4 x 115–175g/4–6oz chump chops, turning over and rearranging once. Leave to stand, covered, for 10 minutes before using.
frozen uncooked joint	per 450g/1lb boned and rolled joint per 450g/1lb joints on bone	DEFROST	To defrost, place joint on a microwaveproof roasting rack or upturned saucer in a dish. Microwave both types of joint for 5–6 minutes per 450g/1lb, turning over once. Leave to stand, covered, for 30–45 minutes, before using.
LIVER			
frozen slices	225g/8oz 450g/1lb	DEFROST	To defrost, spread slices on a plate. Cover and microwave for 4–5 minutes for 225g/8oz; and 8–9 minutes for 450g/1lb, turning twice. Leave to stand, covered, for 5 minutes before using.
PORK			
frozen chops	2 x 115–175g/4–6oz loin 4 x 115–175g/4–6oz loin 2 x 225g/8oz chump 2 x 225g/8oz chump	DEFROST	To defrost, place on a microwaveproof roasting rack and microwave for 3–4 minutes for 2 x 115–175g/4–6oz loin chops; 6–8 minutes for 4 x 115–175g/4–6oz loin chops; 7–9 minutes for 2 x 225g/8oz chump chops; and 14–16 minutes for 4 x 225g/8oz chump chops, turning and rearranging once. Leave to stand for 10 minutes before using.
frozen fillet or tenderloin	350g/12oz per 450g/1lb	DEFROST	To defrost, place on a microwaveproof roasting rack and microwave for 3–4 minutes for a 350g/12oz fillet or tenderloin; and 5–6 minutes per 450g/1lb, turning over once. Leave to stand for 10 minutes before using.
frozen uncooked joint	per 450g/1lb joint on bone per 450g/1lb boneless joints	DEFROST	To defrost, place joint on a microwaveproof roasting rack or upturned saucer in a dish. Microwave both types of joint for 7–8 minutes per 450g/1lb, turning over once. Leave to stand, covered, for 20–45 minutes before using.
SAUSAGEMEAT			
frozen	450g/1lb	DEFROST	To defrost, remove any wrappings and place in a shallow microwaveproof dish. Cover and microwave for 6–8 minutes, breaking up twice. Leave to stand, covered, for 4–5 minutes before using.
SAUSAGES			
frozen	4 standard 8 standard 8 chipolatas 16 chipolatas	DEFROST	To defrost separated or linked sausages, place on a plate, cover and microwave for 3–4 minutes for 4 standard; 5–6 minutes for 8 standard; 3 minutes for 8 chipolatas; and 5 minutes for 16 chipolatas, separating, turning over and rearranging twice. Leave to stand, covered, for 2–5 minutes before using.
VEAL			
frozen chops	2 4 6	DEFROST	To defrost, arrange in a microwaveproof dish so that the thicker portions are to the outer edge. Cover and microwave for 5–6 minutes for 2 chops; 8–10 minutes for 4 chops; and 12–15 minutes for 6 chops, turning and rearranging twice. Leave to stand, covered, for 5–10 minutes before using.
frozen roast	900g/2lb 1.5kg/3–3½lb 1.75kg/4–4½lb 2.25kg/5–5¼lb	DEFROST	To defrost, place in a microwaveproof dish and microwave for 16–18 minutes for a 900g/2lb joint; 24–27 minutes for a 1.5kg/3–3½lb joint; 32–36 minutes for a 1.75kg/4–4½lb joint; and 40–45 minutes for a 2.25kg/5–5¼lb joint, turning twice. Shield any thinner areas with foil as they defrost. Leave to stand, covered, for 10–20 minutes before using.

General Defrosting Chart

BISCUITS frozen	225g/8oz	DEFROST	Arrange in a circle around the edge of a plate. Microwave for 1–1½ minutes, turning over once halfway through cooking. Leave to stand for 5 minutes before serving.
BREAD frozen large white or brown sliced or uncut loaf	800g/1¾lb	DEFROST	Loosen wrapper but do not remove. Microwave for 4 minutes. Leave to stand for 5 minutes before slicing or removing ready-cut slices. Leave a further 10 minutes before serving.
frozen individual bread slices and rolls	1 slice/1 roll 2 slices/2 rolls 4 slices/4 rolls	DEFROST	Wrap loosely in kitchen paper and microwave for ¼–½ minute for 1 slice/1 roll; ½–1 minute for 2 slices/2 rolls; and 1½–2 minutes for 4 slices/4 rolls. Leave to stand for 2 minutes before serving.
frozen pitta bread	2 4	DEFROST	Place on a double thickness piece of kitchen paper and microwave for 1½–2 minutes for 2 pittas; and 2–3 minutes for 4 pittas, turning once halfway through the cooking time.
frozen crumpets	2 4	HIGH	To defrost *and* reheat. Place on a double thickness piece of kitchen paper and microwave for ½–¾ minute for 2 crumpets; 1–1½ minutes for 4 crumpets, turning once.
CAKES frozen small light fruit cake	small light fruit cake 1 slice	DEFROST	To defrost, place on a microwaveproof rack and microwave, uncovered, for 5 minutes for a whole small cake; ½–¾ minute for 1 slice, rotating twice. Leave to stand for 10 minutes before serving.
frozen Black Forest gâteau	15cm/6in gâteau	DEFROST	To defrost, place on a serving plate and microwave, uncovered, for 4–6 minutes, checking constantly. Leave to stand for 30 minutes before serving.
frozen cream sponge	15cm/6in sponge	HIGH	To defrost, place on a double thickness piece of kitchen paper and microwave for 45 seconds. Leave to stand for 10–15 minutes before serving.
frozen jam sponge	15–18cm/6–7in sponge	DEFROST	To defrost, place on a double thickness piece of kitchen paper and microwave for 3 minutes. Leave to stand for 5 minutes before serving.
frozen small sponge buns	2 4	DEFROST	To defrost, place on a rack and microwave for 1–1½ minutes for 2 buns; and 1½–2 minutes for 4 buns, checking frequently. Leave to stand for 5 minutes before serving.
frozen chocolate éclairs	2	DEFROST	To defrost, place on a double thickness sheet of kitchen paper and microwave for ¾–1 minute. Leave to stand 5–10 minutes before serving.
frozen doughnuts	2 x cream filled 2 x jam filled	DEFROST	To defrost, place on a double thickness sheet of kitchen paper and microwave for 1–1½ minutes for 2 cream-filled doughnuts; and 1½–2 minutes for 2 jam-filled doughnuts. Leave to stand 3–5 minutes before serving.
CASSEROLES frozen	2 servings 4 servings	HIGH	To defrost *and* reheat. Place in a microwaveproof dish, cover and microwave for 8–10 minutes for 2 servings; 14–16 minutes for 4 servings, breaking up and stirring twice as the casserole thaws. Leave to stand, covered, for 3–5 minutes before serving.
CHEESECAKE frozen	individual fruit-topped individual cream-topped family-size fruit-topped family-size cream-topped	DEFROST	To defrost, remove from container and place on a microwaveproof serving plate. Microwave for 1–1½ minutes for individual fruit-topped; 1–1¼ minutes for individual cream-topped; 5–6 minutes for family-size fruit-topped; and 1½–2 minutes for family-size cream-topped, rotating once and checking frequently. Leave to stand for 5–15 minutes before serving.

CREPES OR PANCAKES frozen	8	MEDIUM	To defrost, place a stack of 8 crêpes or pancakes on a plate and microwave for 1½–2 minutes, rotating once. Leave to stand for 5 minutes, then peel apart to use.
CROISSANTS frozen	2 4	DEFROST	To defrost, place on a double thickness piece of kitchen paper and microwave for ½–1 minute for 2 croissants; and 1½–2 minutes for 4 croissants.
FISH IN SAUCE frozen boil-in-the bag	1 x 170g/6oz 2 x 170g/6oz	DEFROST *or* MEDIUM	To defrost *and* cook, pierce the bag and place on a plate. Microwave for 11–12 minutes on DEFROST for 1 x 170g/6oz bag; and 10–12 minutes on MEDIUM for 2 x 170g/6oz bags. Shake gently to mix, leave to stand for 2 minutes then snip open to serve.
FLANS & QUICHES frozen unfilled cooked flans	15–18cm/6–7in	DEFROST	To defrost, place on a plate and microwave for 1–1½ minutes. Leave to stand for 5 minutes before using.
frozen filled cooked flans	10cm/4in 20cm/8in	HIGH	To defrost *and* cook, place on a plate and microwave for 1–1½ minutes for a 10cm/4in flan; and 2½–3½ minutes for a 20cm/8in flan. Leave to stand for 5 minutes before serving or using.
FRUIT CRUMBLE frozen cooked frozen uncooked	made with 900g/2lb prepared fruit and 175g/6oz crumble topping (to serve 4)	DEFROST *then* HIGH	To defrost *and* cook, microwave frozen cooked crumble for 15 minutes on DEFROST, then 5 minutes on HIGH; and frozen uncooked crumble for 15 minutes on DEFROST, then 10–14 minutes on HIGH, until cooked or reheated.
LASAGNE frozen prepared	450g/1lb	DEFROST *then* HIGH	To defrost *and* cook, remove any foil packaging and place in a microwave-proof dish. Cover and microwave on DEFROST for 8 minutes. Allow to stand for 5 minutes, then microwave on HIGH for 8–9 minutes. Brown under a preheated hot grill if liked.
ORANGE JUICE frozen concentrated	175ml/6fl oz carton	HIGH	To defrost, remove lid and place in a microwaveproof jug. Microwave for 1–1½ minutes, stirring once. Add water to dilute and serve.
PASTA frozen cooked	275g/10oz	DEFROST	To defrost *and* reheat, place in a microwaveproof dish, cover and microwave for 10 minutes, stirring twice. Leave to stand, covered, for 2–3 minutes before serving.
PASTRY frozen shortcrust and puff	200g/7oz packet 400g/14oz packet	DEFROST	Do not remove from wrappings unless unsuitable for microwave. Microwave for 2½–3 minutes for a 200g/7oz packet; and 4 minutes for a 400g/14oz packet. Leave to stand for 3 minutes before using.
PATE frozen	115g/4oz pack 200g/7oz pack 275g/10oz slice	DEFROST	Unwrap and place on a plate or leave in dish if suitable for microwave. Cover and microwave for 1 minute for 115g/4oz pack; 3–4 minutes for 200g/7oz pack; and 3–4 minutes for 275g/10oz slice, rotating 2–3 times. Leave to stand for 15–20 minutes before serving.
PIZZA frozen	30cm/12in 13cm/5in	HIGH	To defrost *and* cook. Place on a plate and microwave for 3–5 minutes for a 30cm/12in pizza; and 1½–2 minutes for a 13cm/5in pizza, rotating the dish twice.
RICE frozen cooked	225g/8oz 450g/1lb	HIGH	To defrost *and* reheat. Place in a microwaveproof dish, cover and microwave for 5–6 minutes for 225g/8oz; and 7–8 minutes for 450g/1lb, stirring twice. Leave to stand, covered, for 2 minutes before using.

SCONES frozen	2 4	DEFROST	To defrost, place on a double thickness piece of kitchen paper. Microwave for 1¼–1½ minutes for 2 scones; 3 minutes for 4 scones, rearranging once.
SOUPS frozen	300ml/½ pint/1¼ cups 600ml/1 pint/2½ cups	HIGH	To defrost *and* reheat. Place in a bowl, cover and microwave for 4–4½ minutes for 300ml/½ pint/1¼ cups; and 7–7½ minutes for 600ml/1 pint/2½ cups, breaking up and stirring 2–3 times.
STOCKS frozen	300ml/½ pint/1¼ cups 600ml/1 pint/2½ cups	HIGH	Place in a jug or bowl, microwave uncovered: 2½–3 minutes for 300ml/½ pint/1¼ cups; and 5–6 minutes for 600ml/1 pint/2½ cups, stirring and breaking up 2–3 times.
WHITE SAUCE frozen and variations (such as cheese, parsley or mustard)	300ml/½ pint/1¼ cups	HIGH	To defrost *and* reheat. Place in a microwaveproof dish and microwave for 4–5 minutes, stirring twice. Whisk to serve.
YOGURT frozen	150g/5oz carton	HIGH	To defrost, remove lid and microwave for 1 minute. Stir well and leave to stand for 1–2 minutes before serving.

Strawberry and Hazelnut Roulade.

Index